Miles & Steps

Miles & Steps is the books **790 Miles** and **79,000 Steps**
together in one volume.

790 Miles is 44 photographs from
a drive across mostly rural southern Idaho and back,
790 miles, 35 hours,
during September 2024.

79,000 Steps is 44 photographs from
walks in New York City
(mostly mid to lower Manhattan)
during August 2022.

Published by Imaginary Dynamics
imaginarydynamics.com
ISBN: 978-1-971080-03-1

First Edition
File version 1 4 Z 362

There are no disclaimers, warranties, safety notices,
captions, or guarantees for this book or for anything in life.

Miles & Steps

Otto Kitsinger

790 Miles

A drive across southern Idaho and back,
790 miles,
35 hours,
in chronological order.

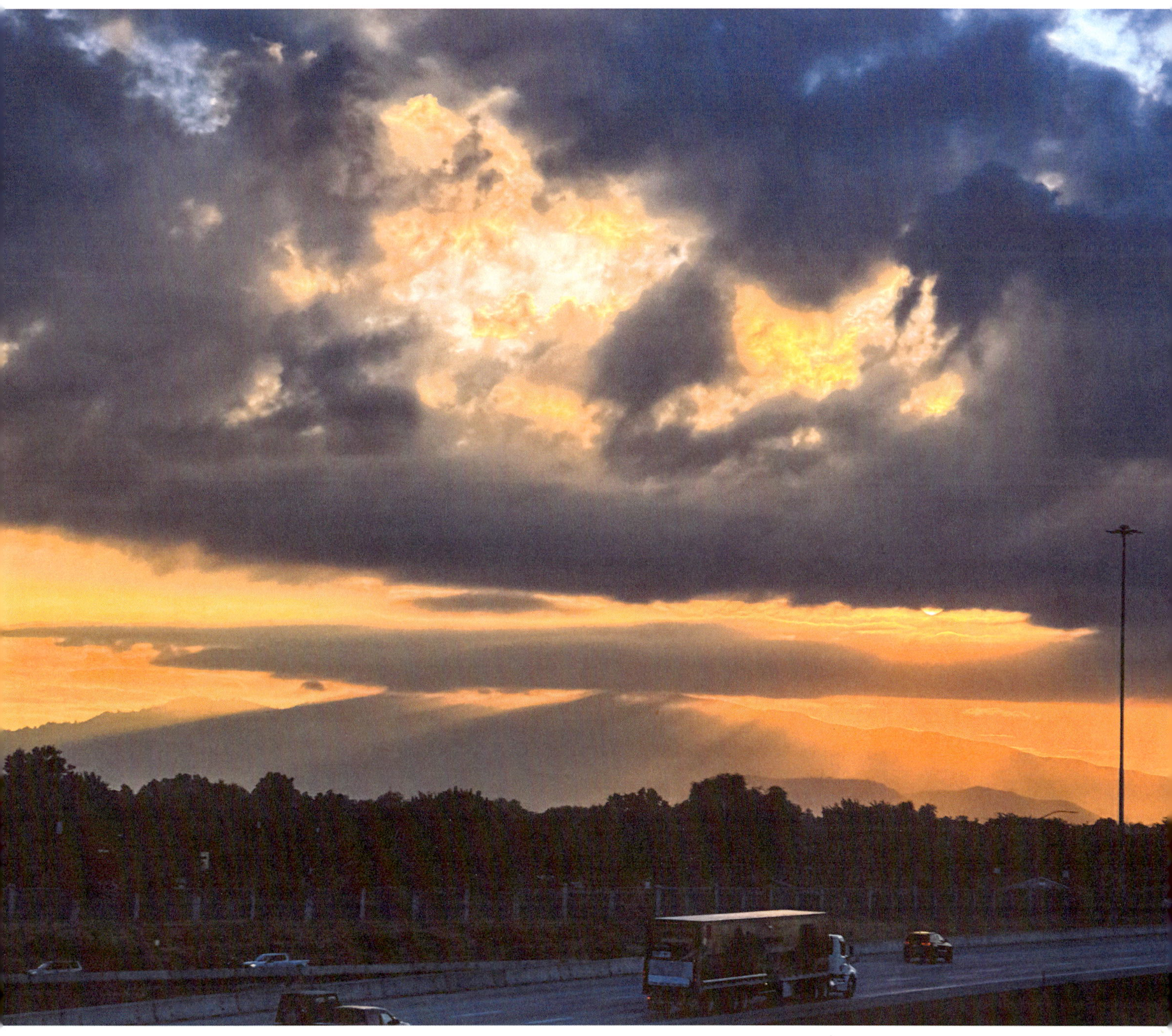

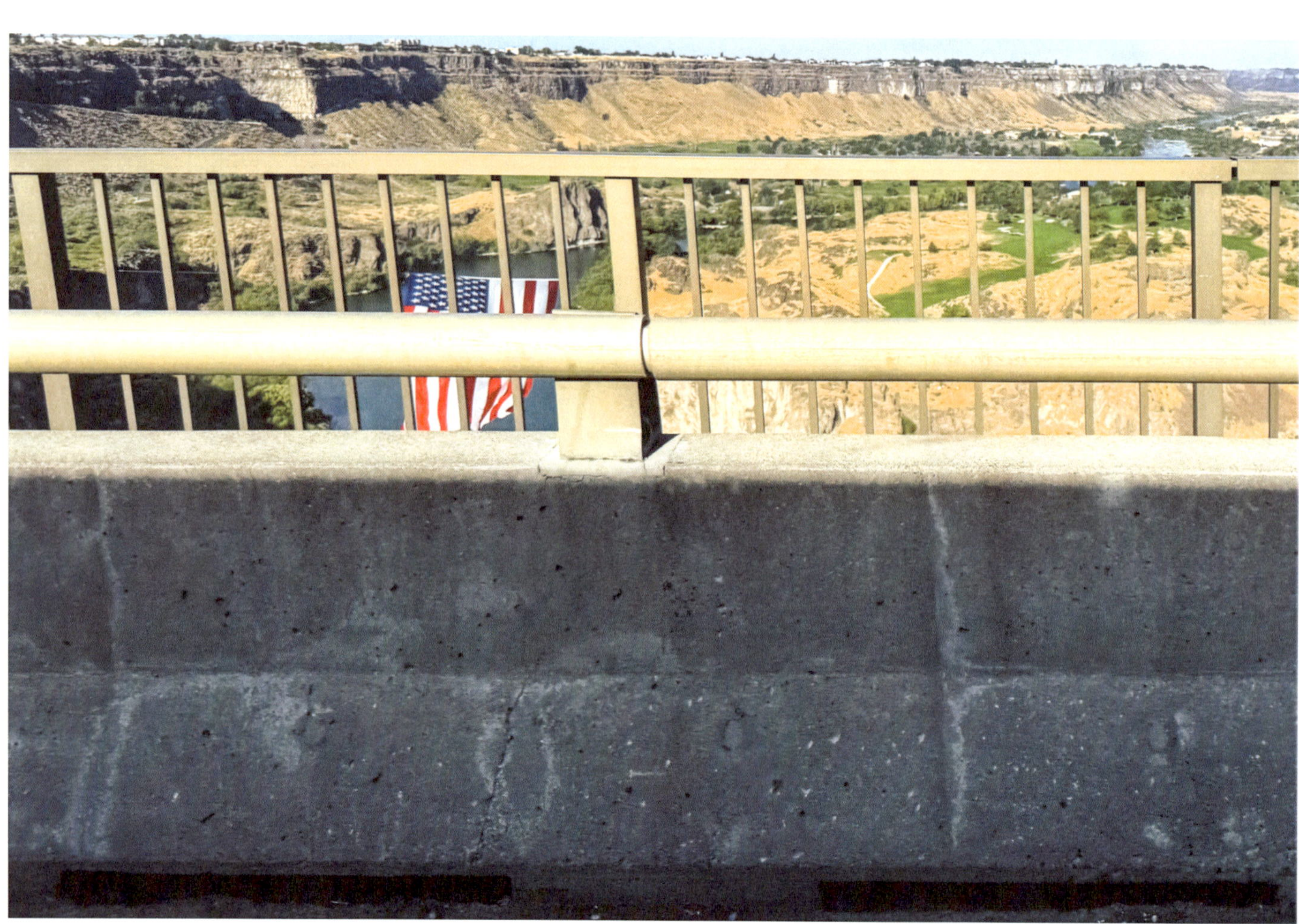

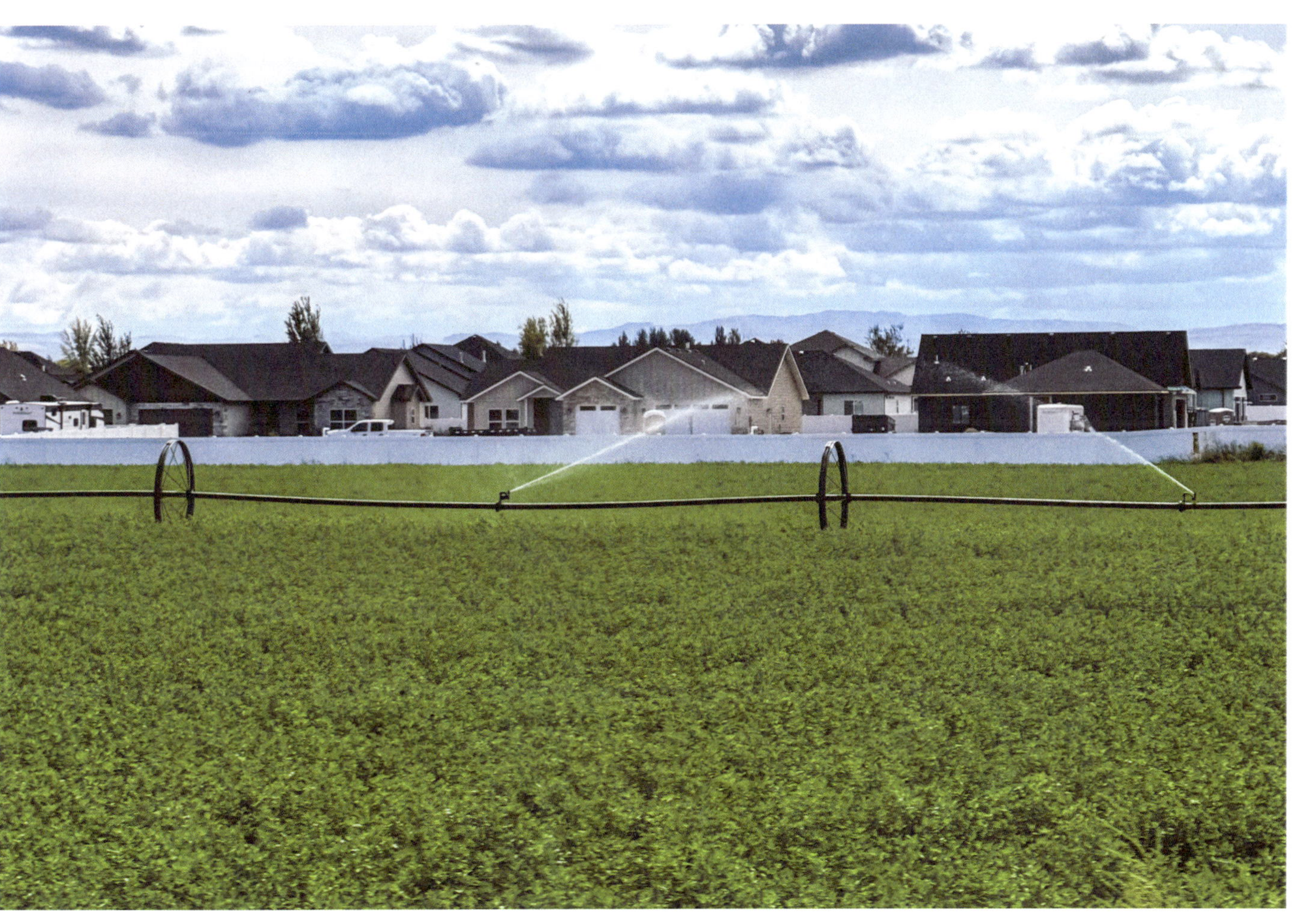

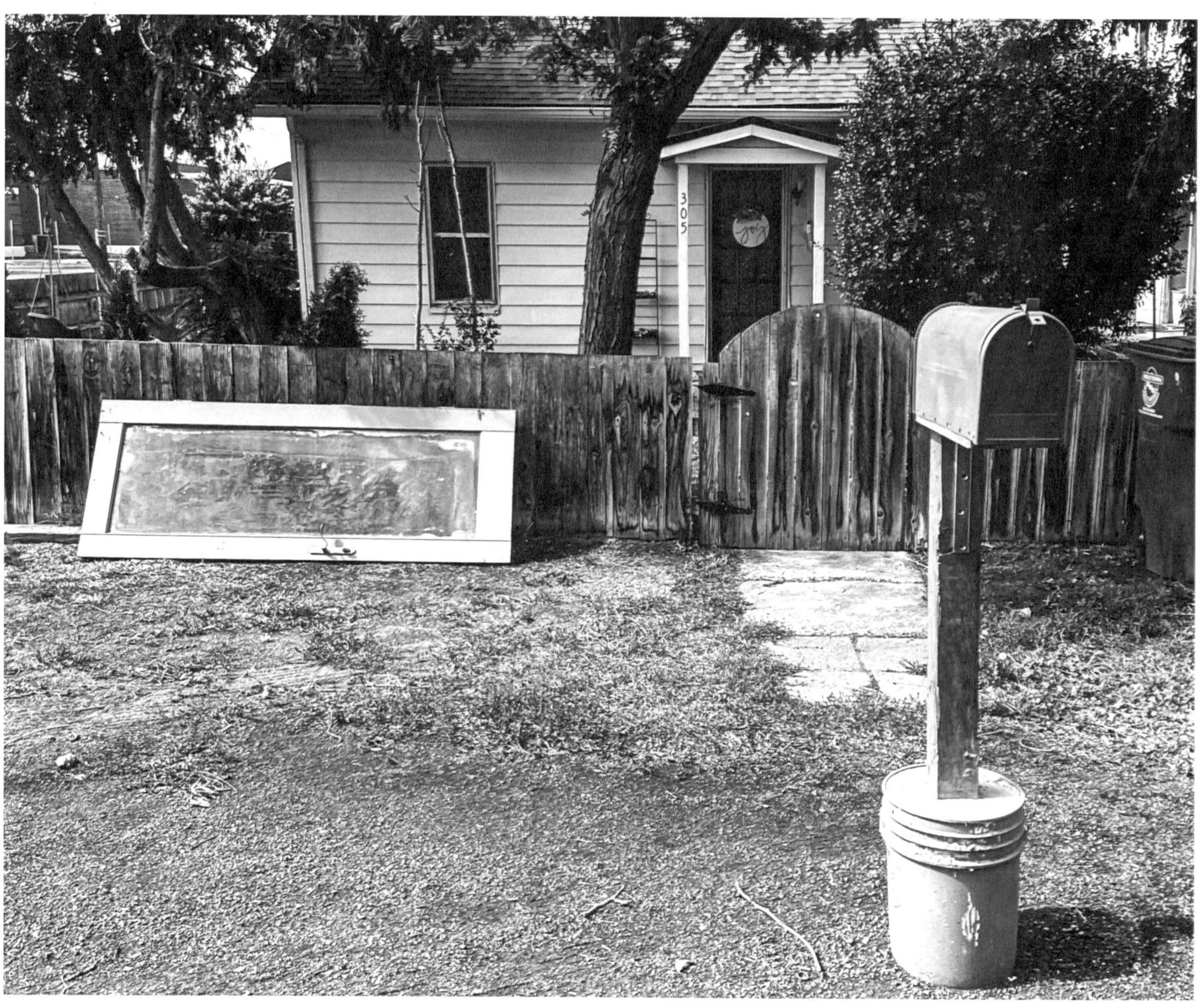

305

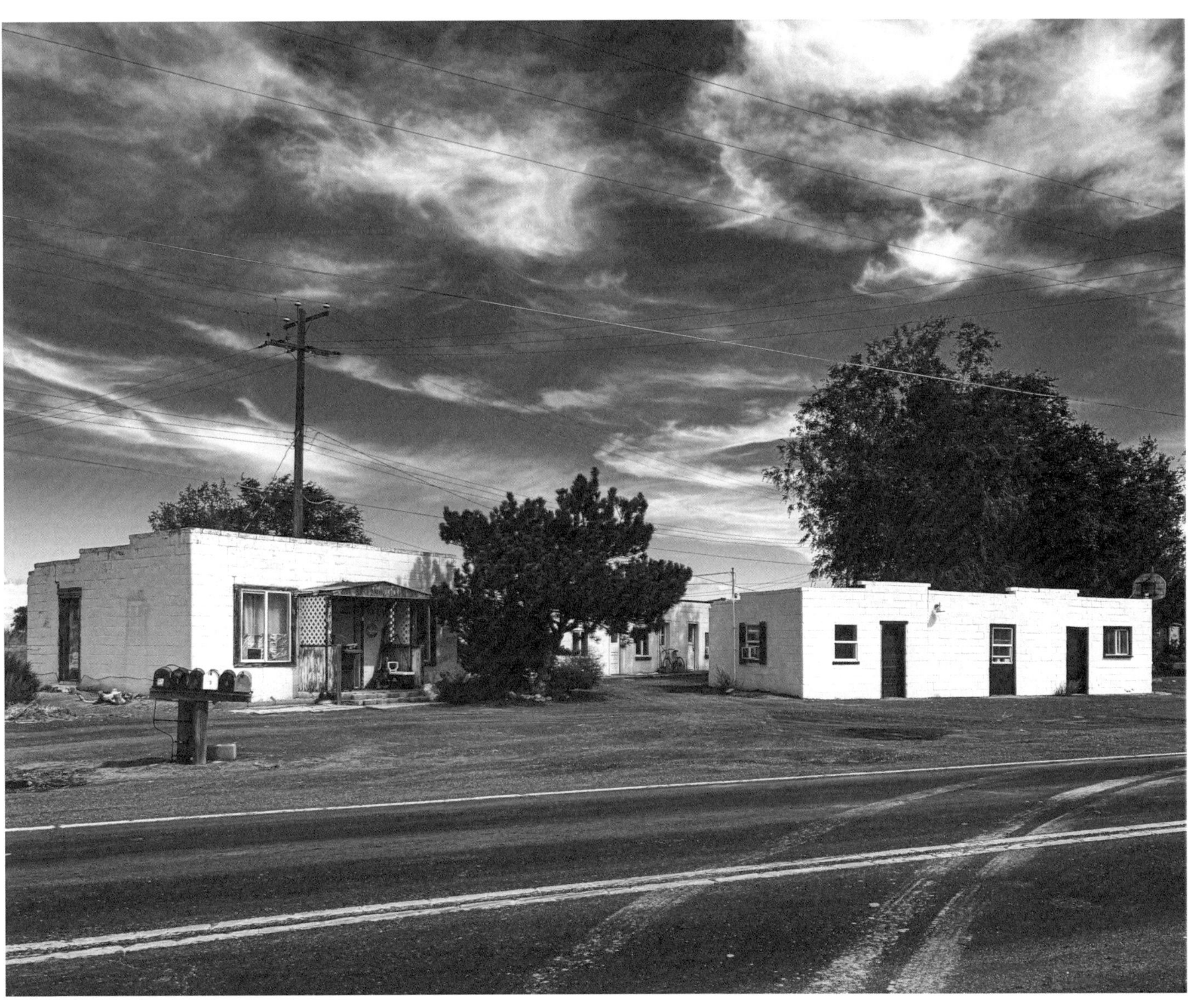

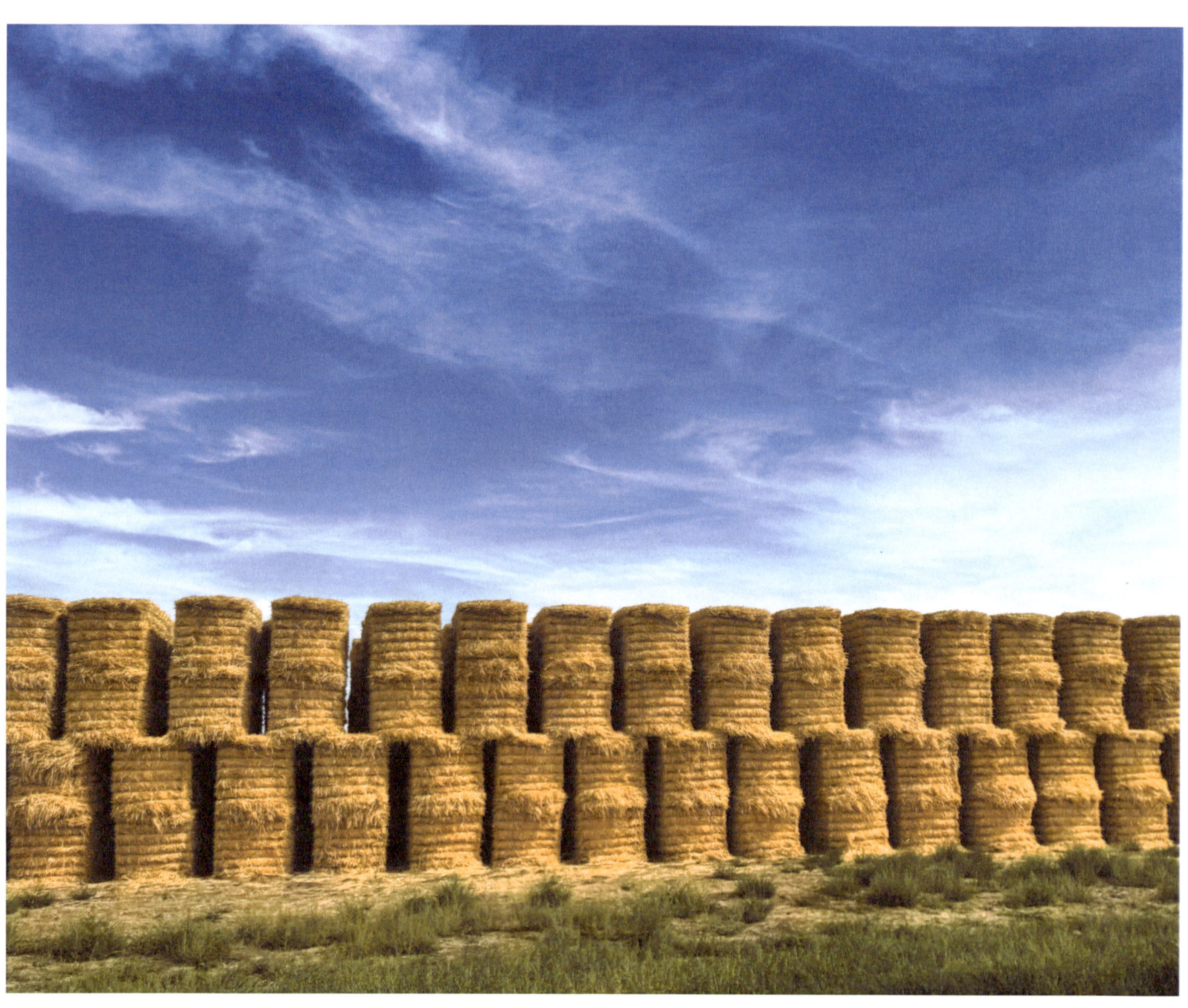

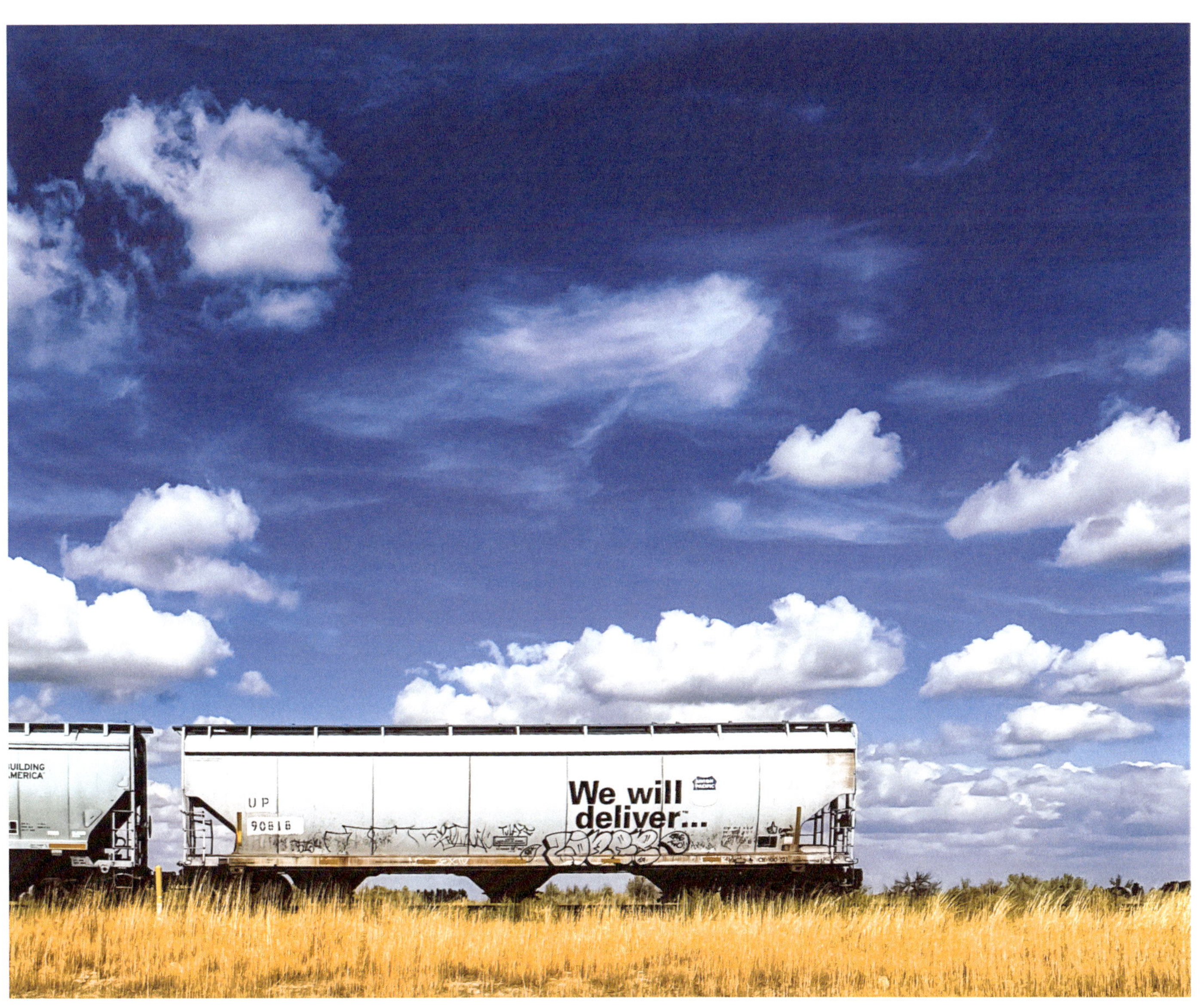
BUILDING
AMERICA
U P
90816
We will
deliver...

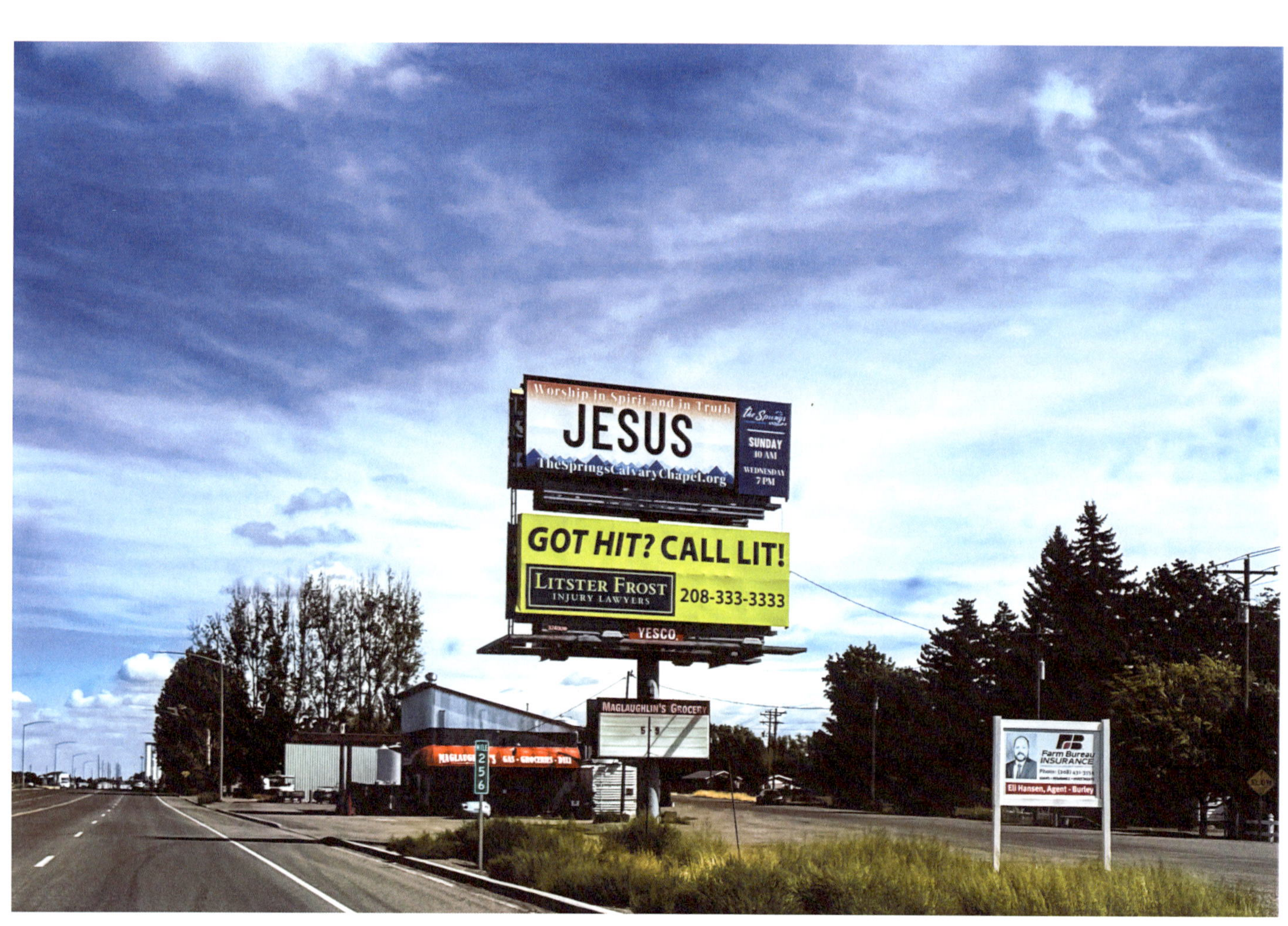

Worship in Spirit and in Truth
The Springs
JESUS
SUNDAY
10 AM
WEDNESDAY
7 PM
TheSpringsCalvaryChapel.org
GOT HIT? CALL LIT!
LITSTER FROST
INJURY LAWYERS
208-333-3333
YESCO
MAGLAUGHLIN'S GROCERY
MILE 256
Farm Bureau INSURANCE
Eli Hansen, Agent - Burley

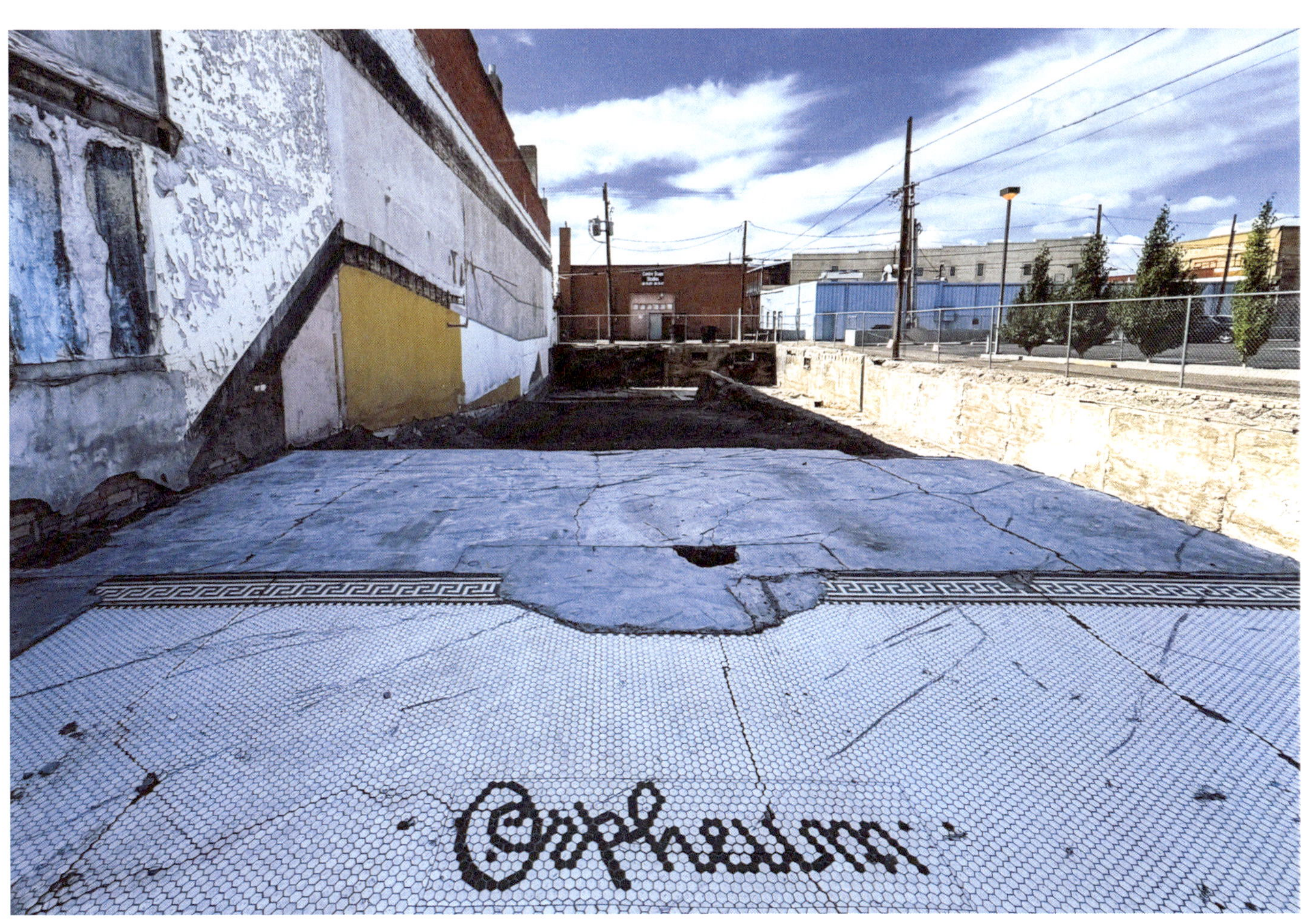

Orpheum

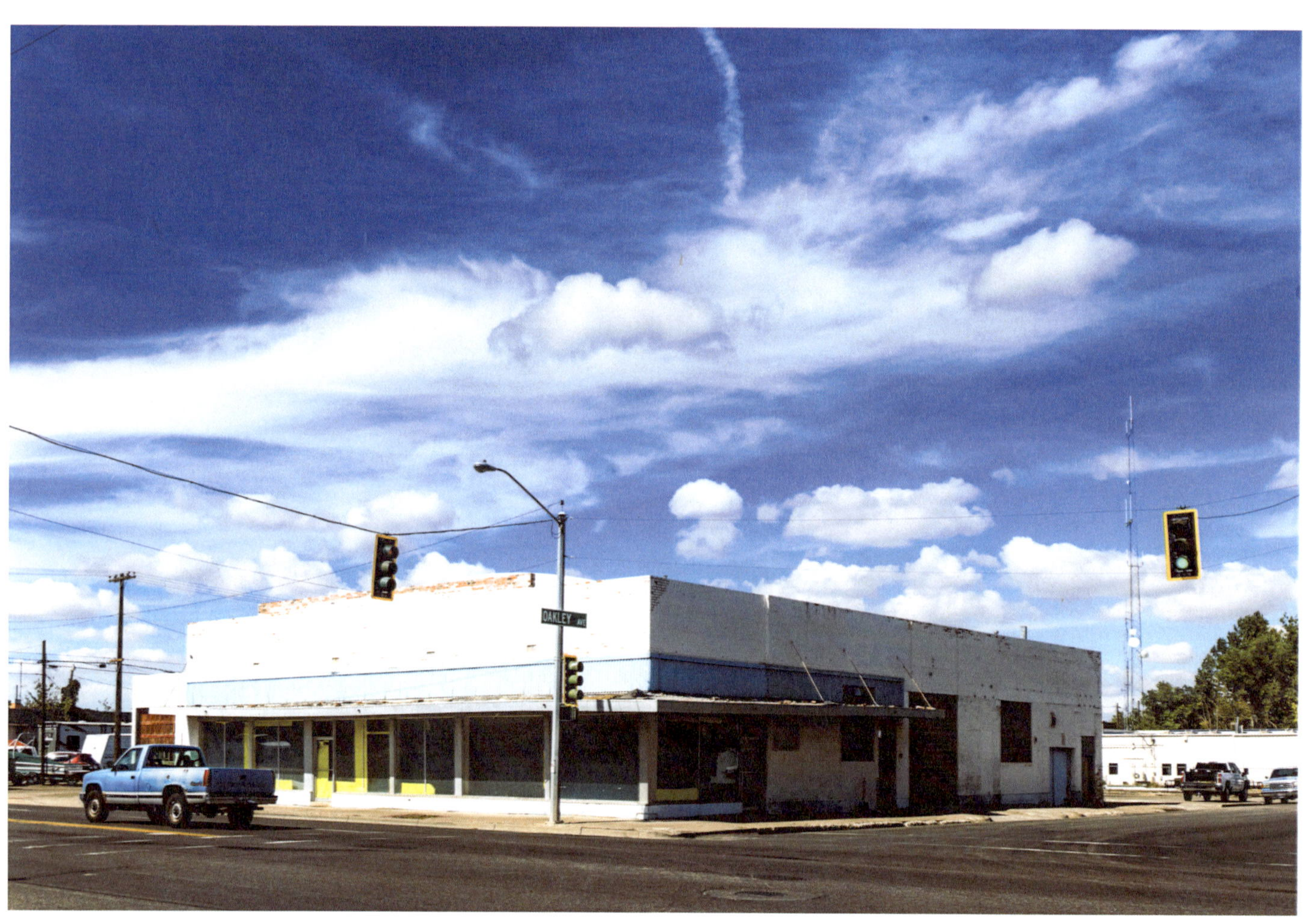
OAKLEY AVE

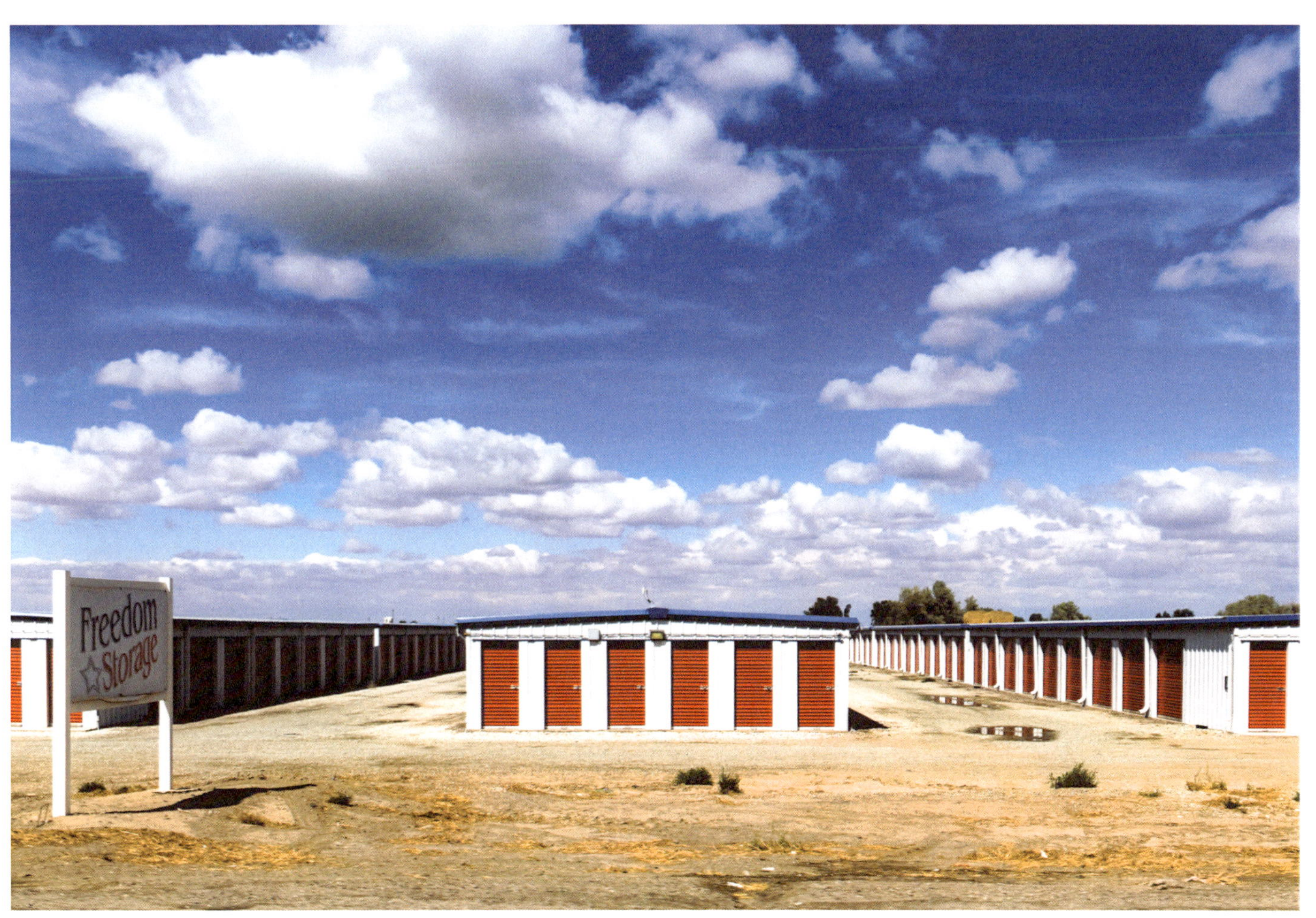

Freedom
Storage

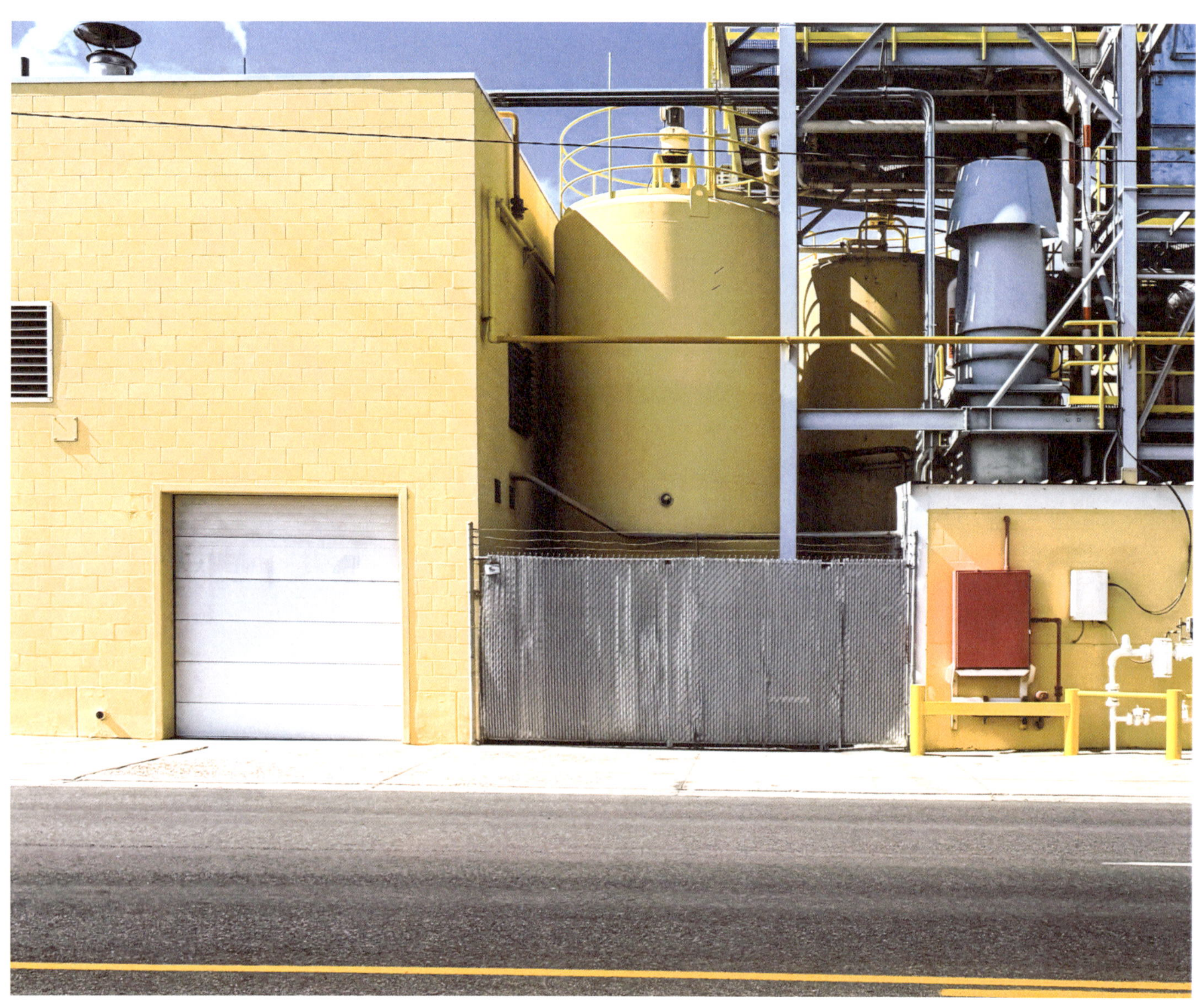

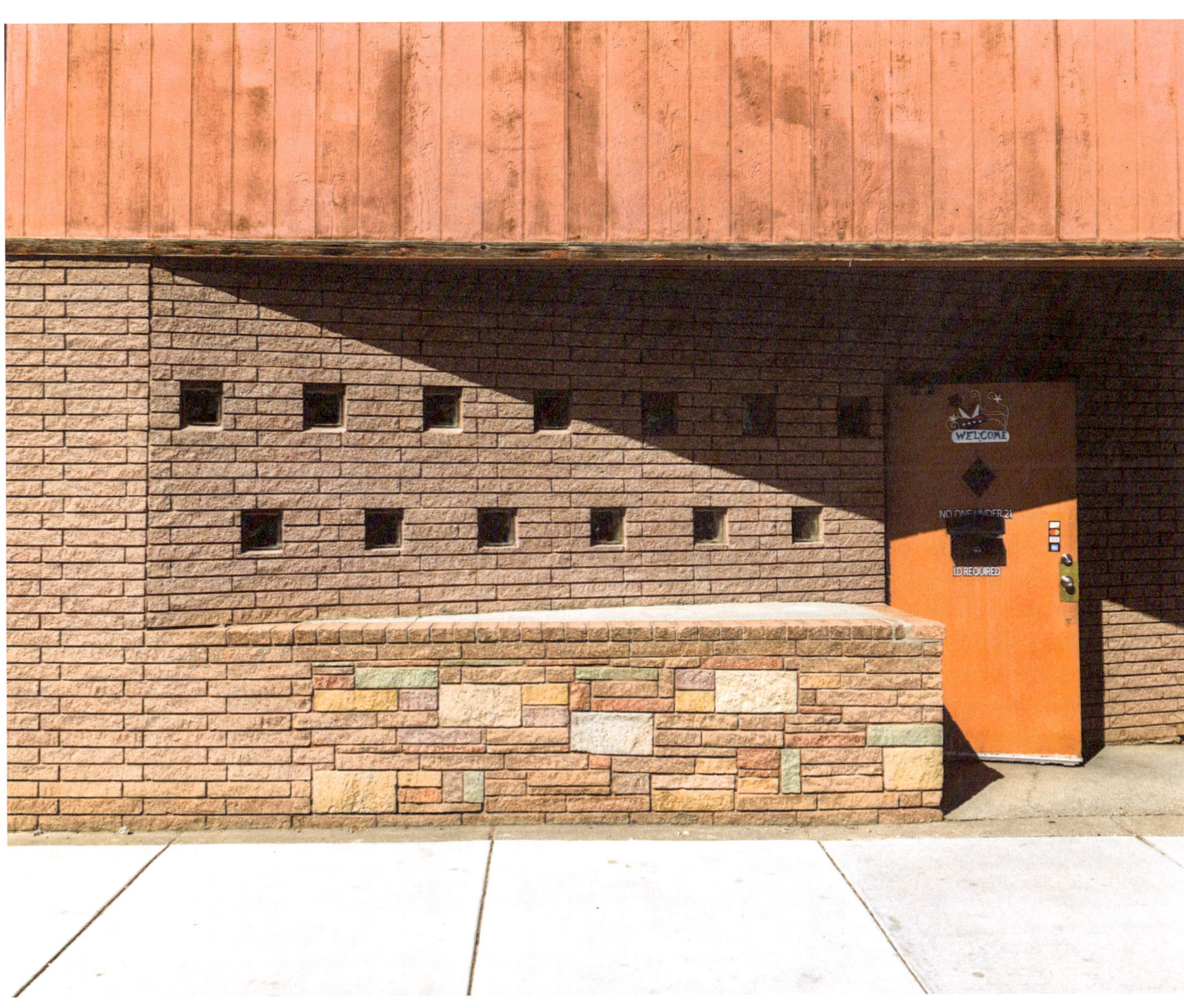
WELCOME
NO ONE UNDER 21
ID REQUIRED

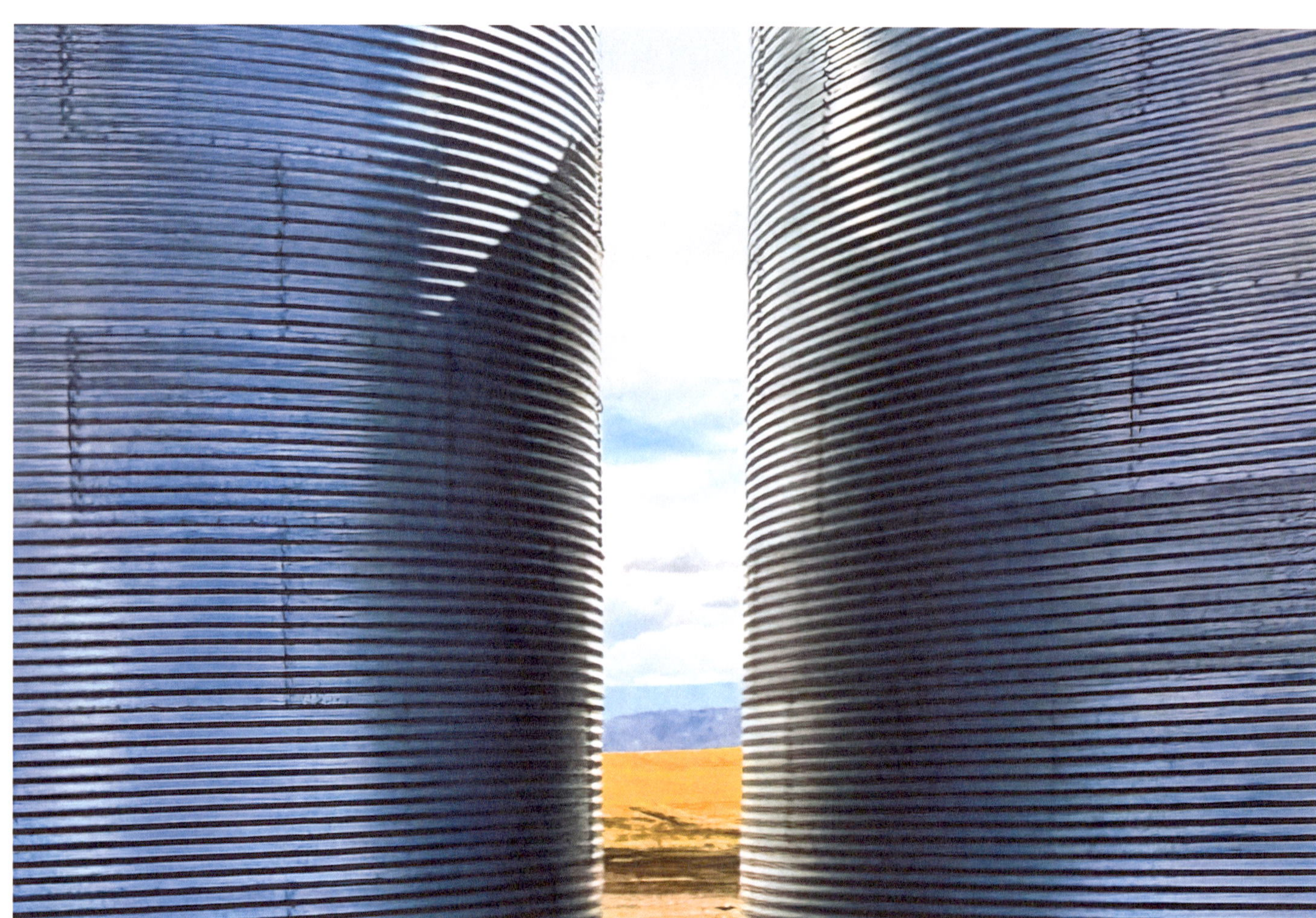

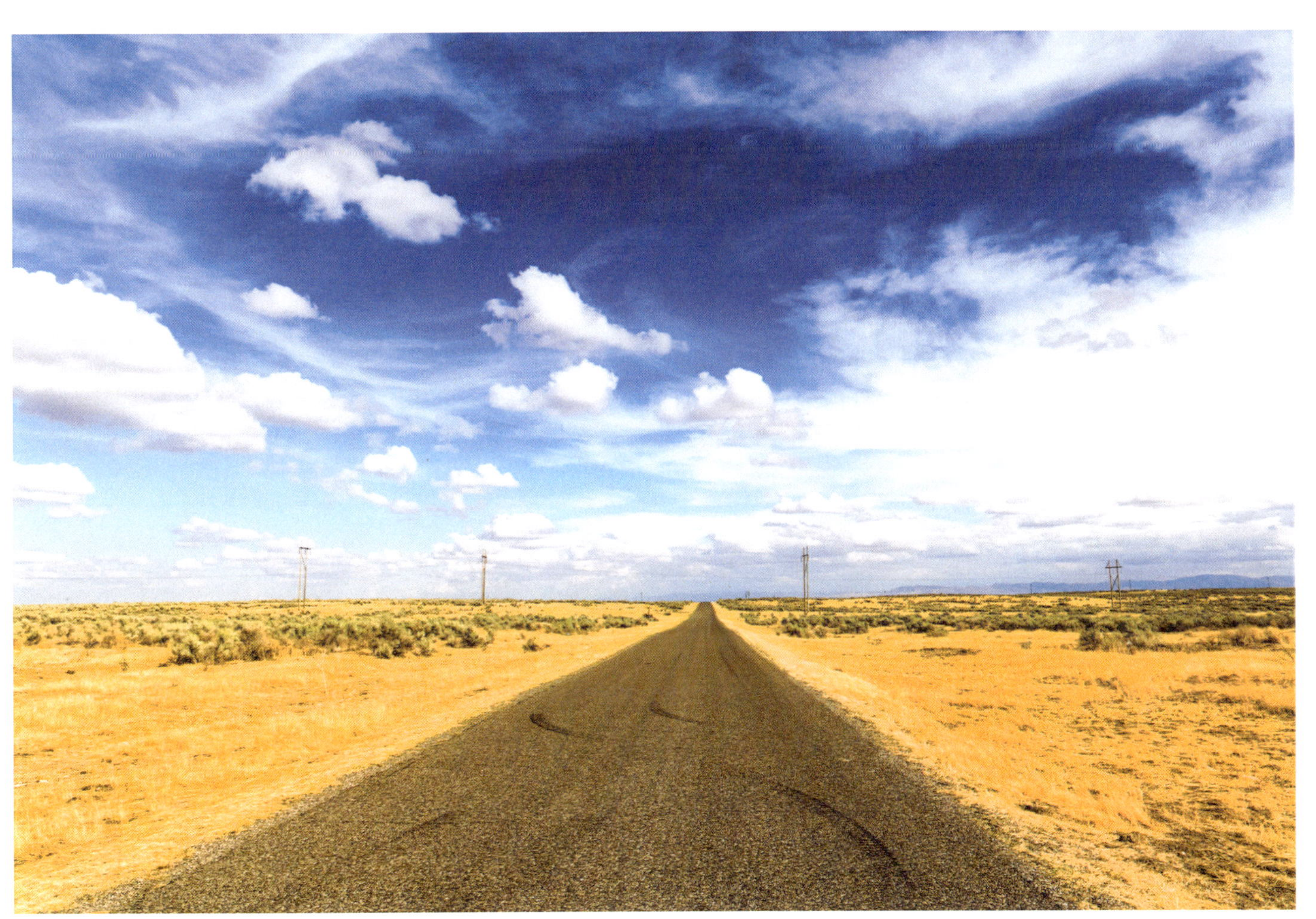

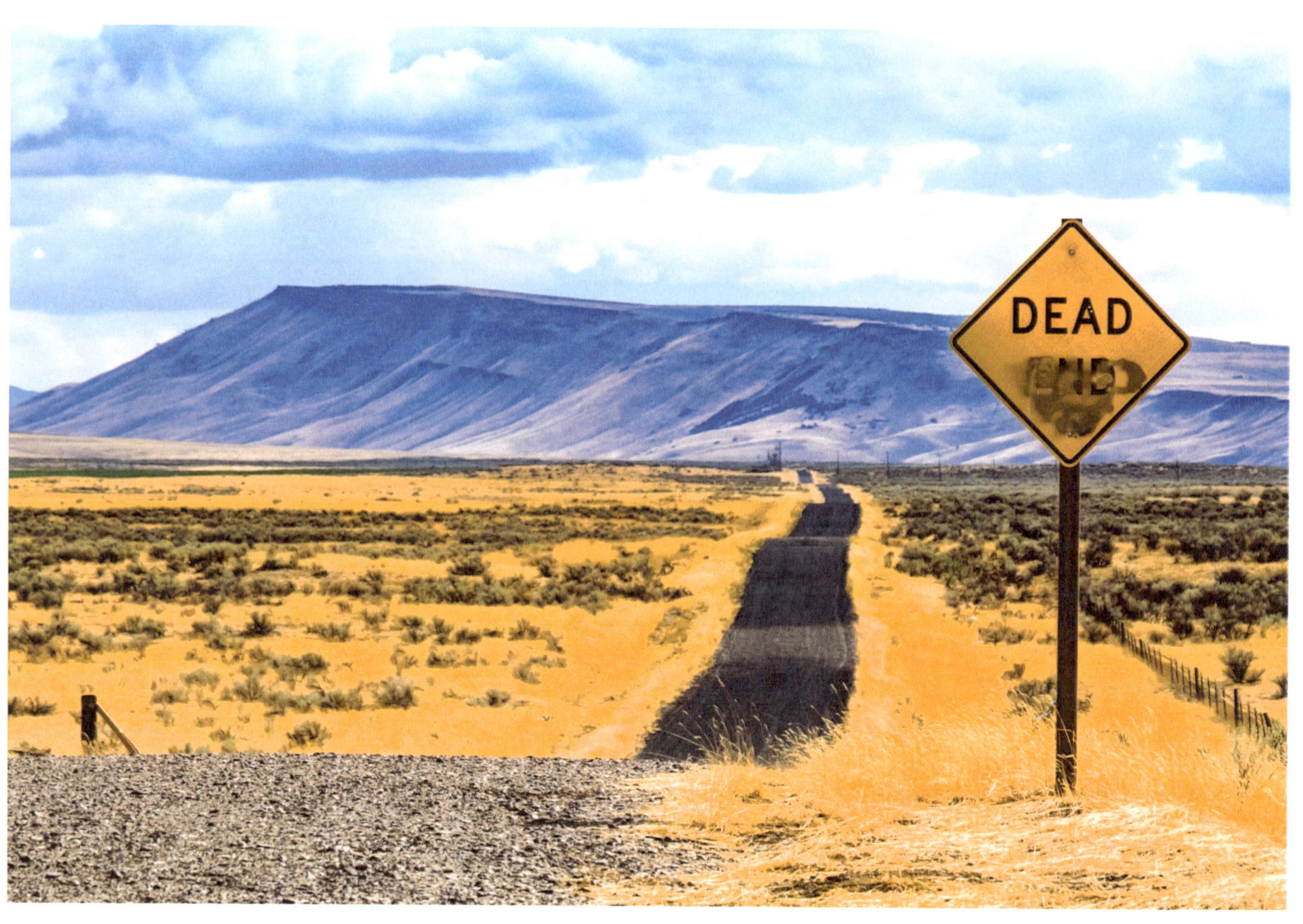

DEAD
END

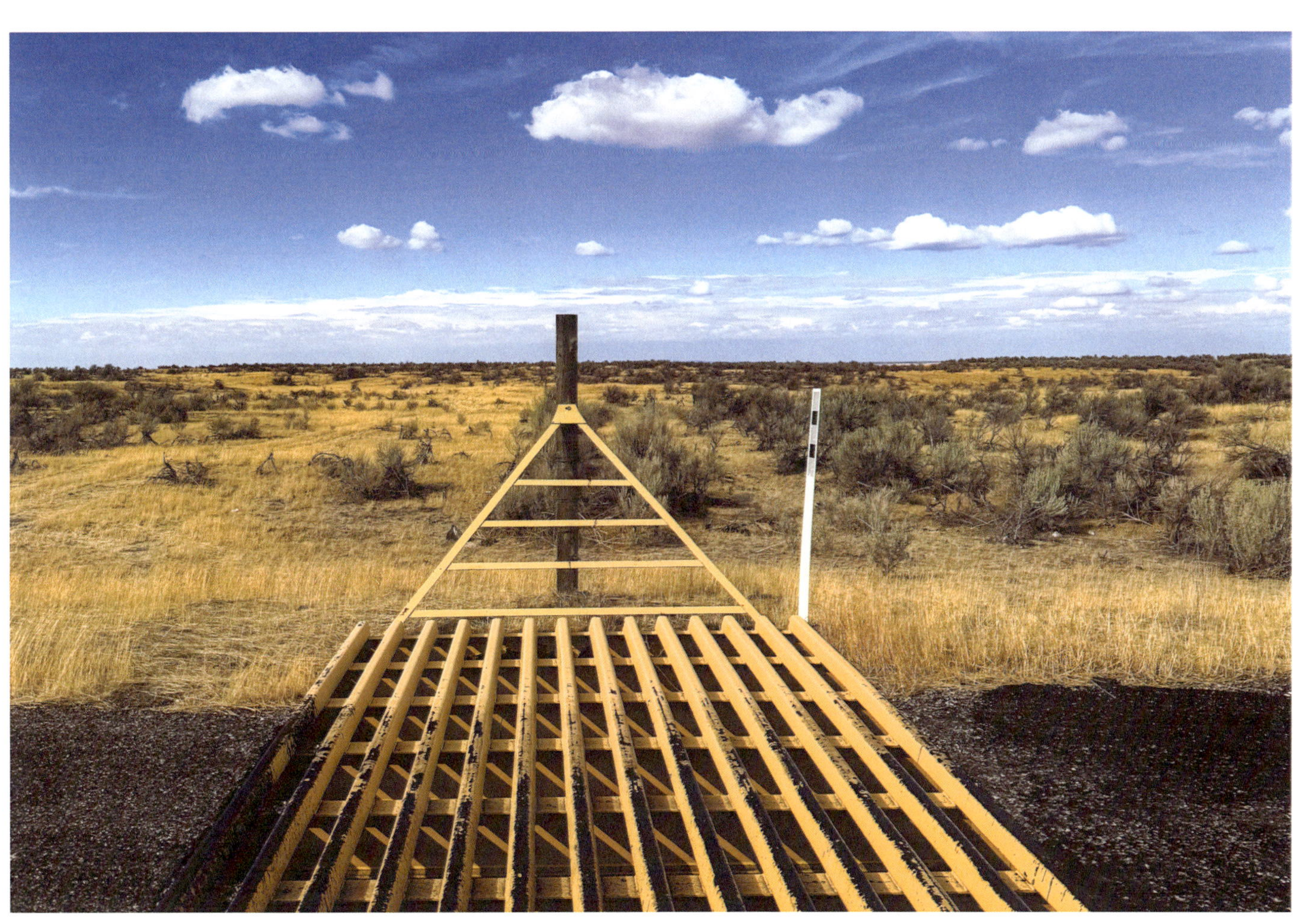

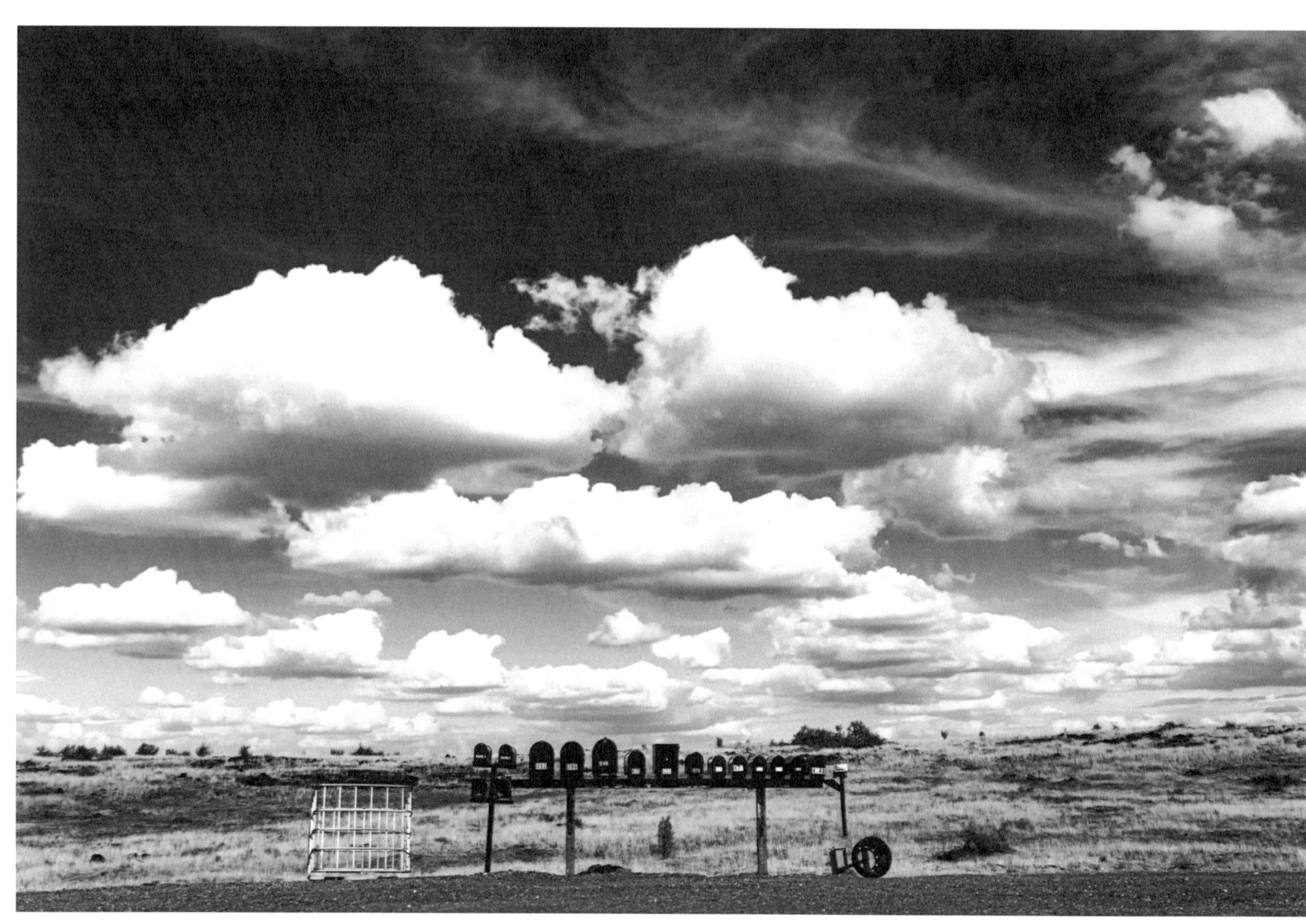

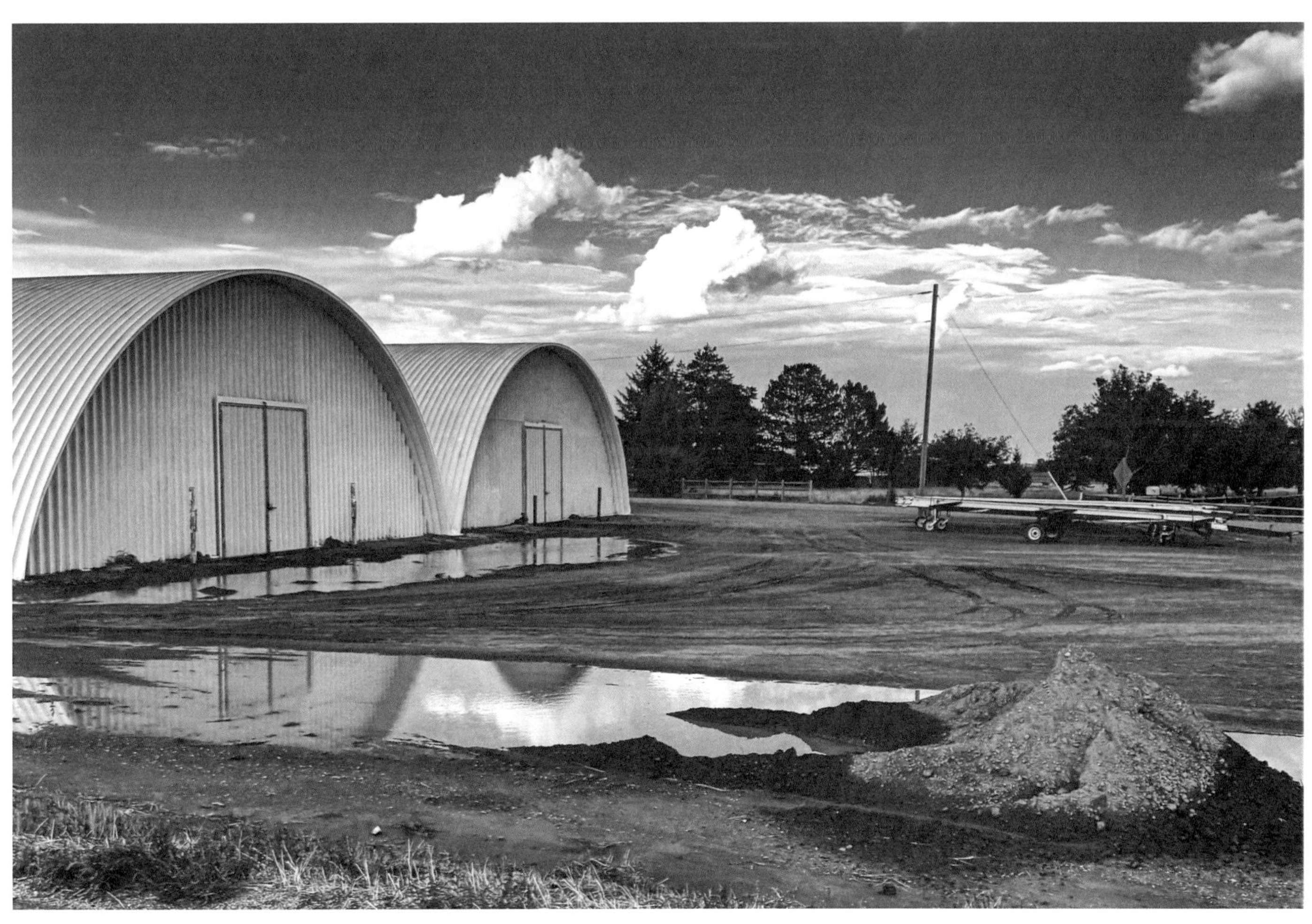

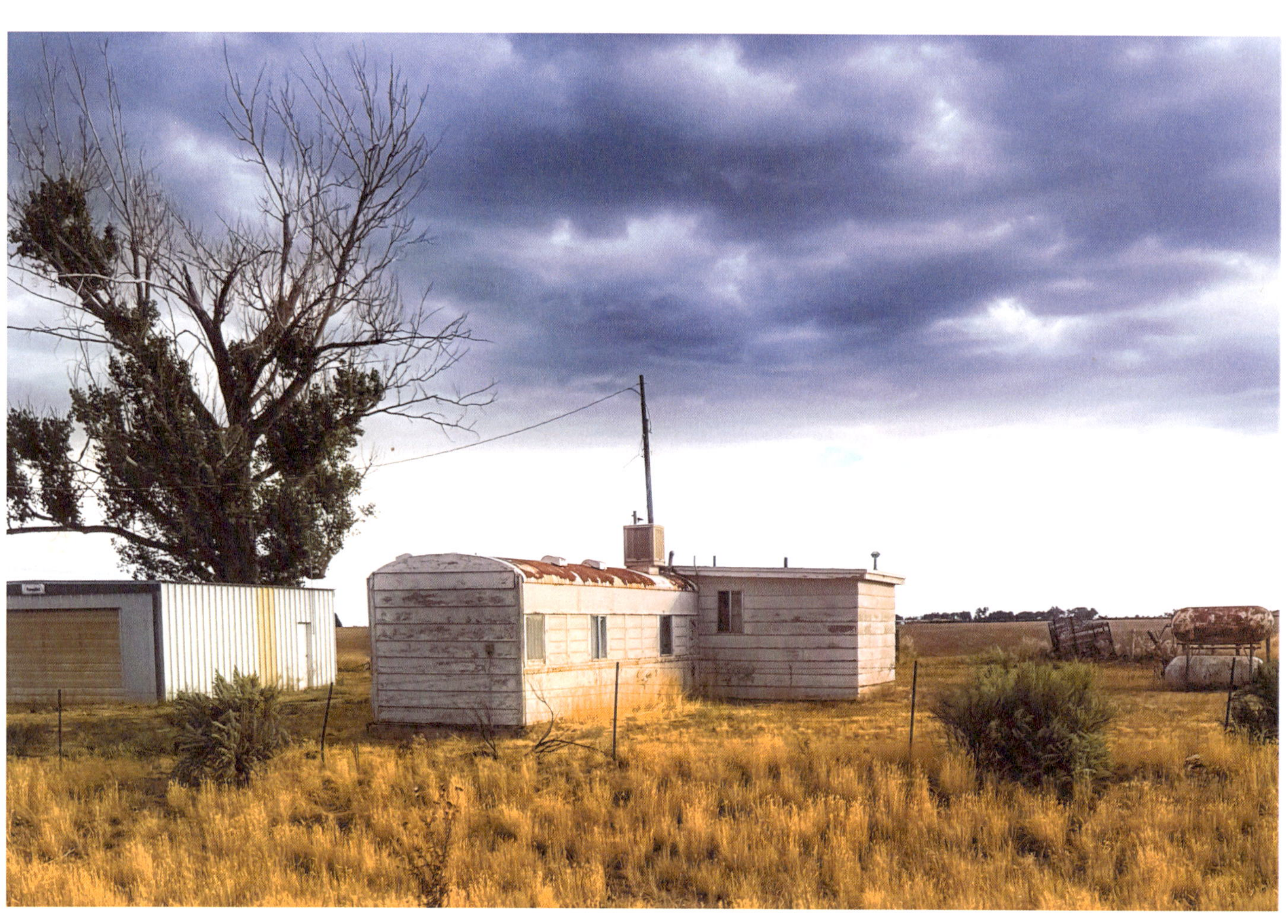

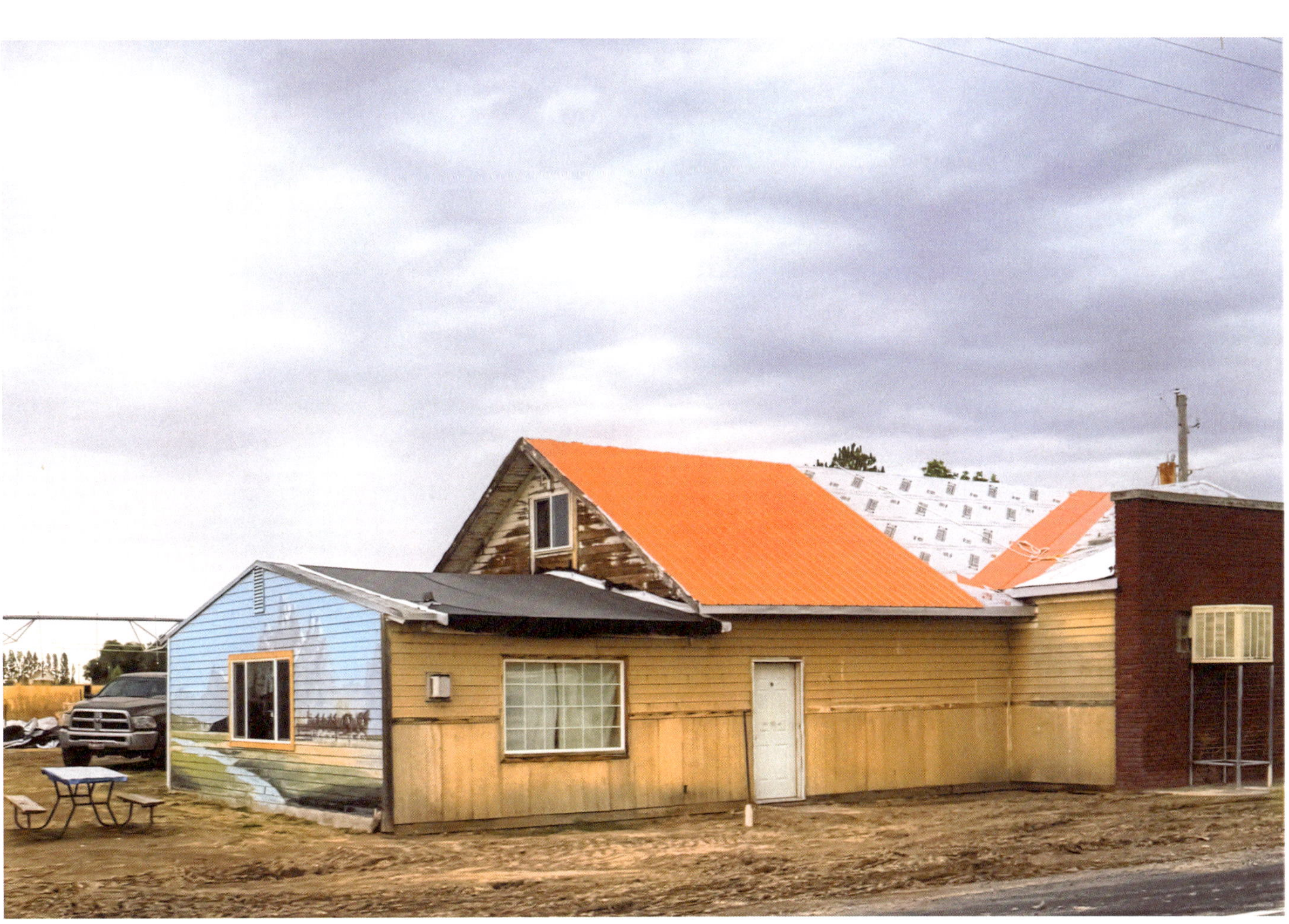

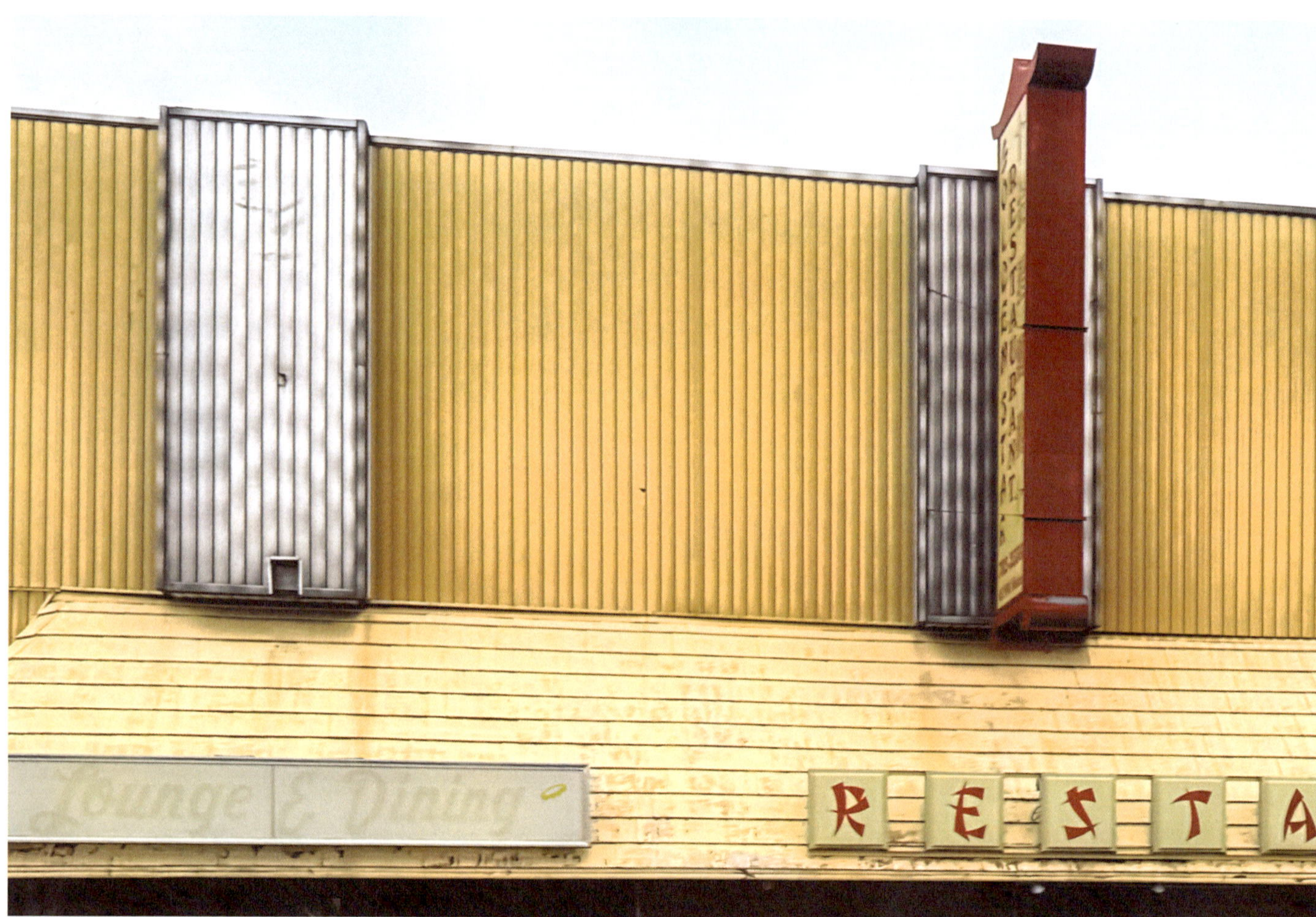
Lounge & Dining
RESTA

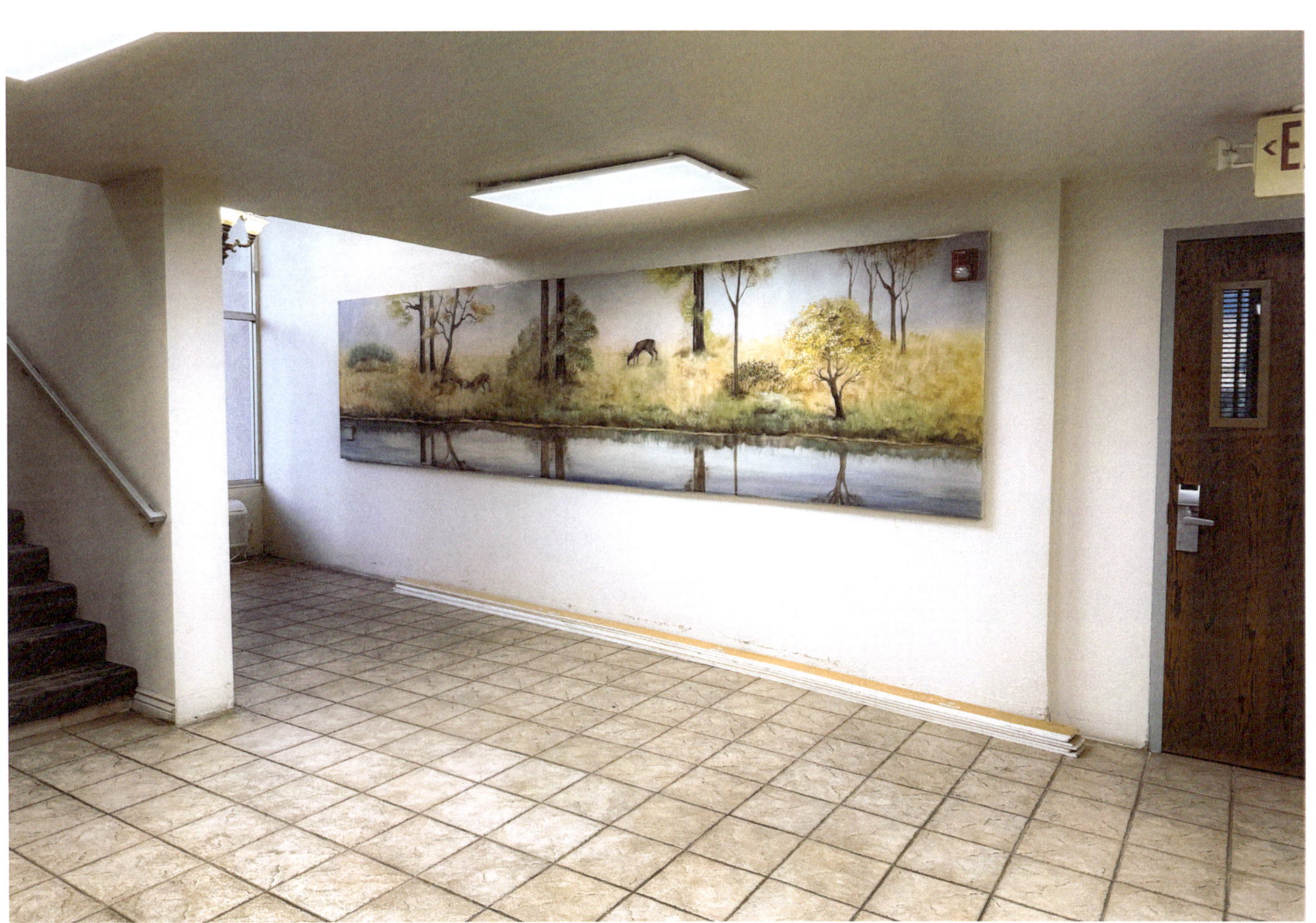

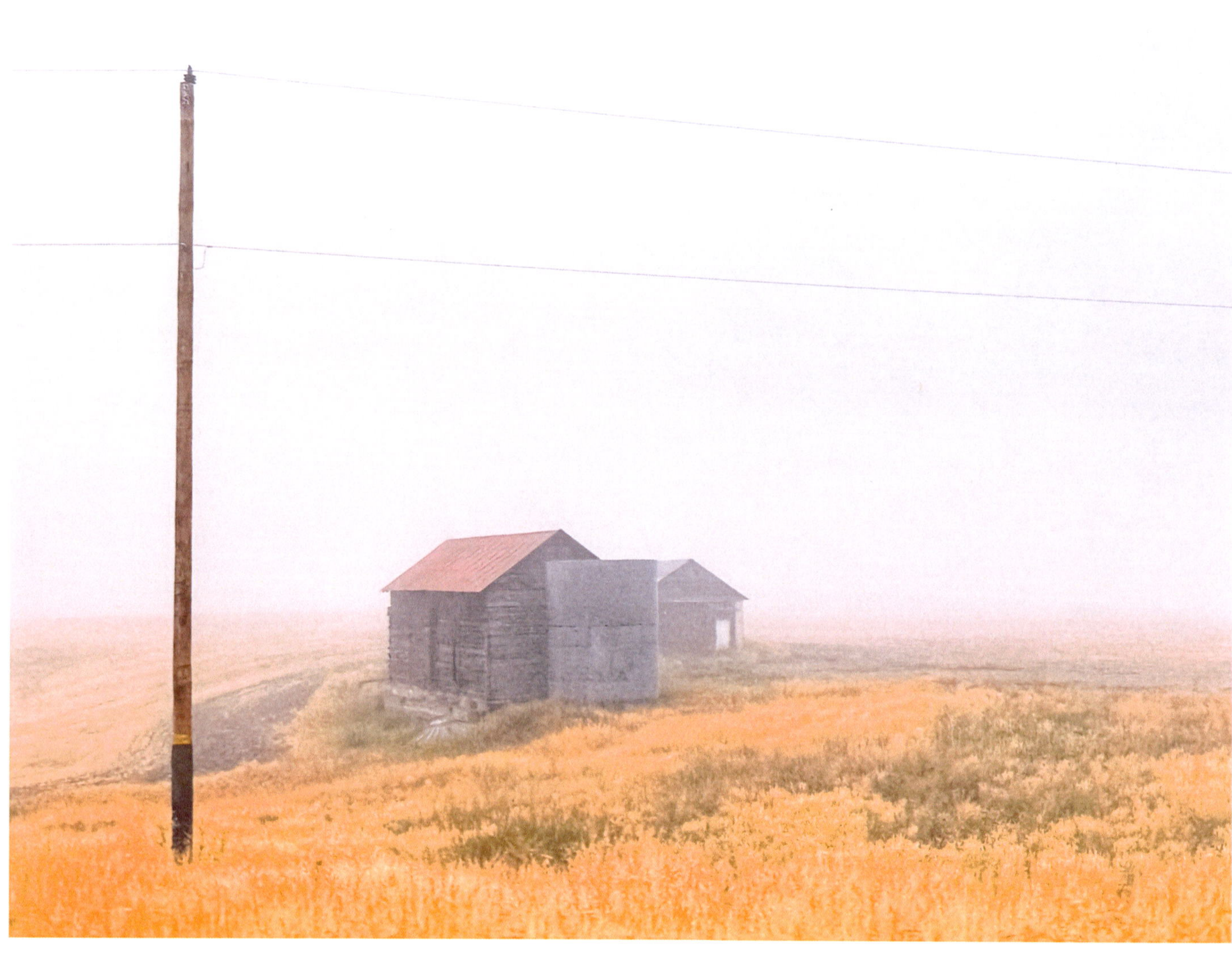

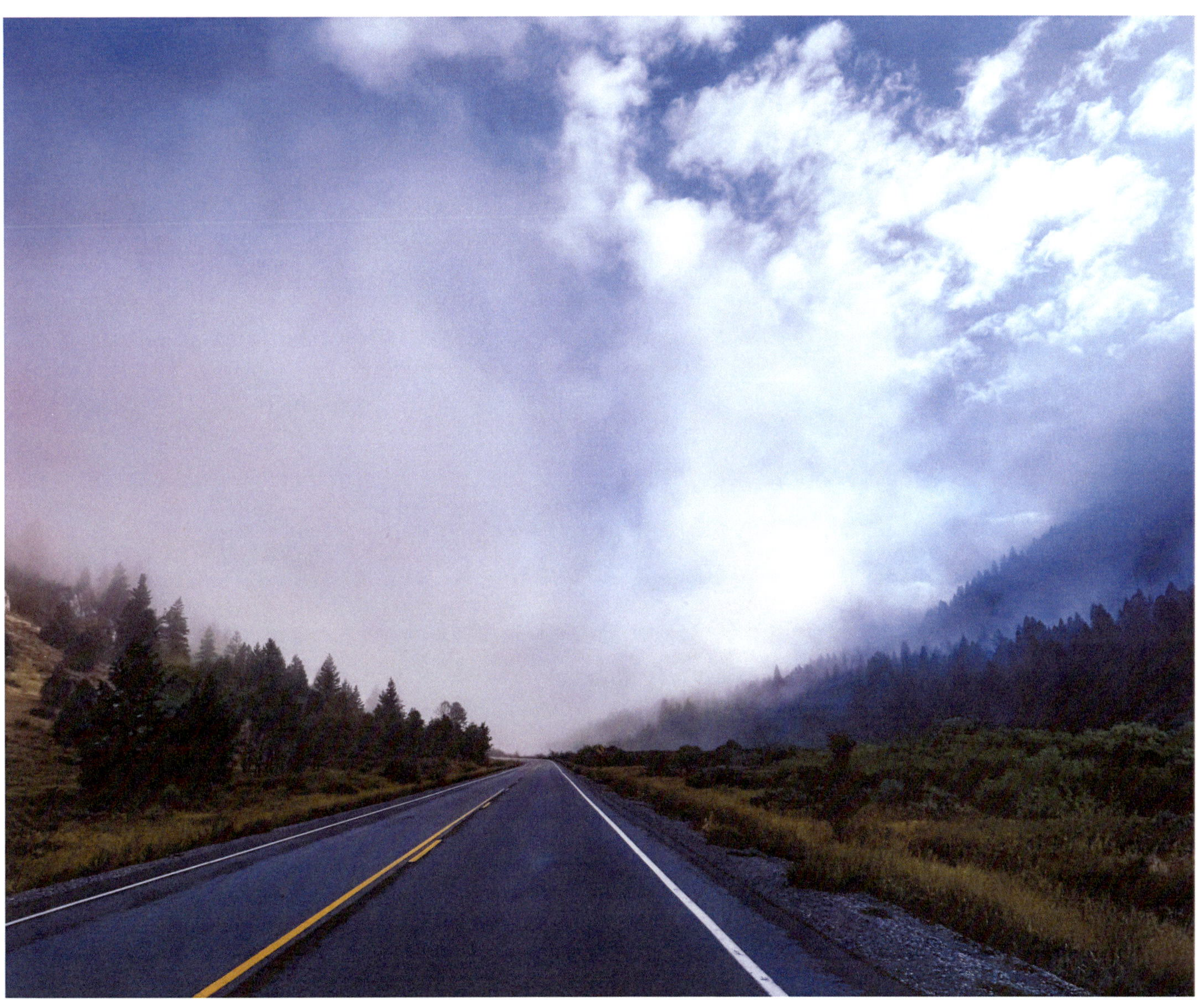

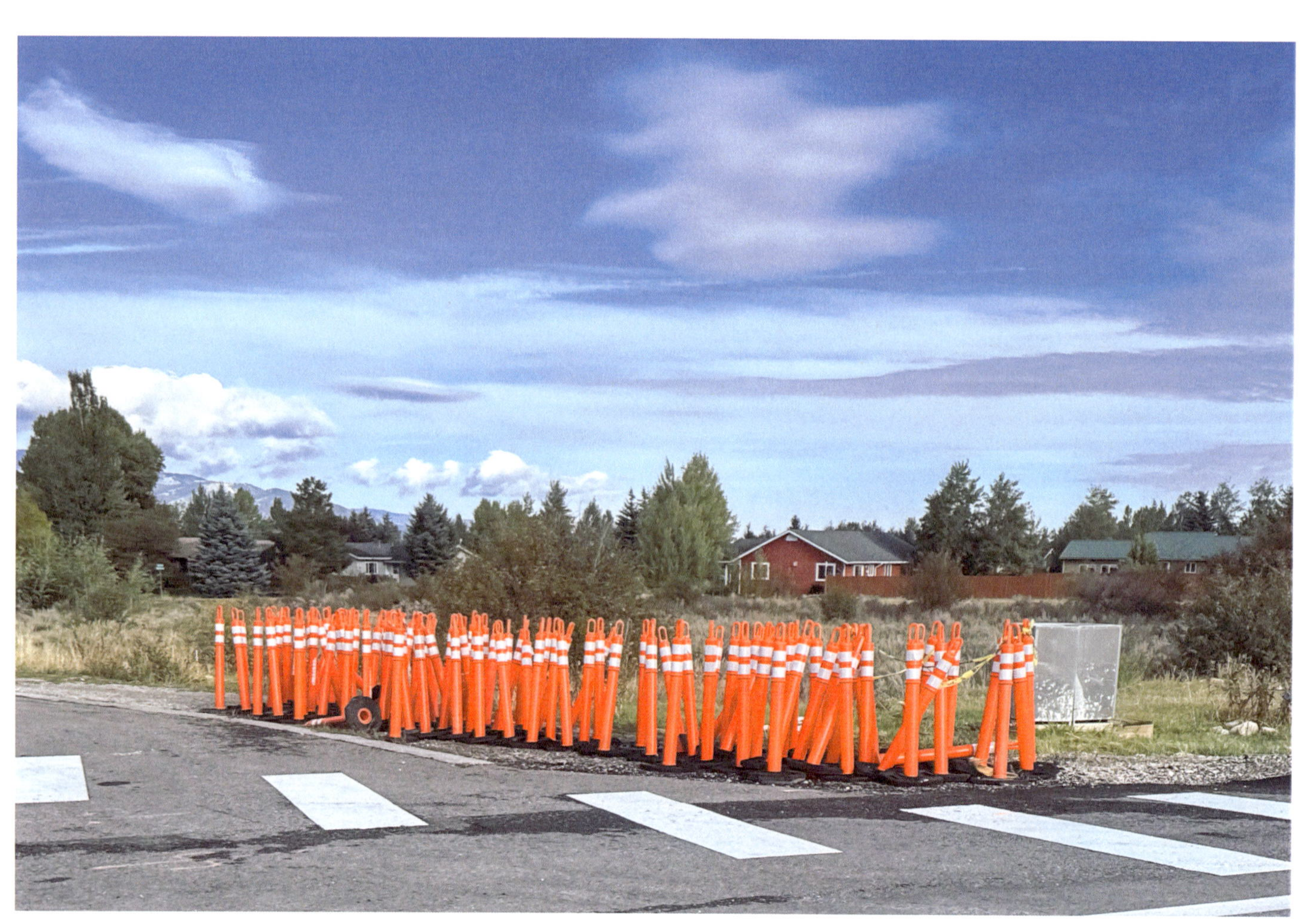

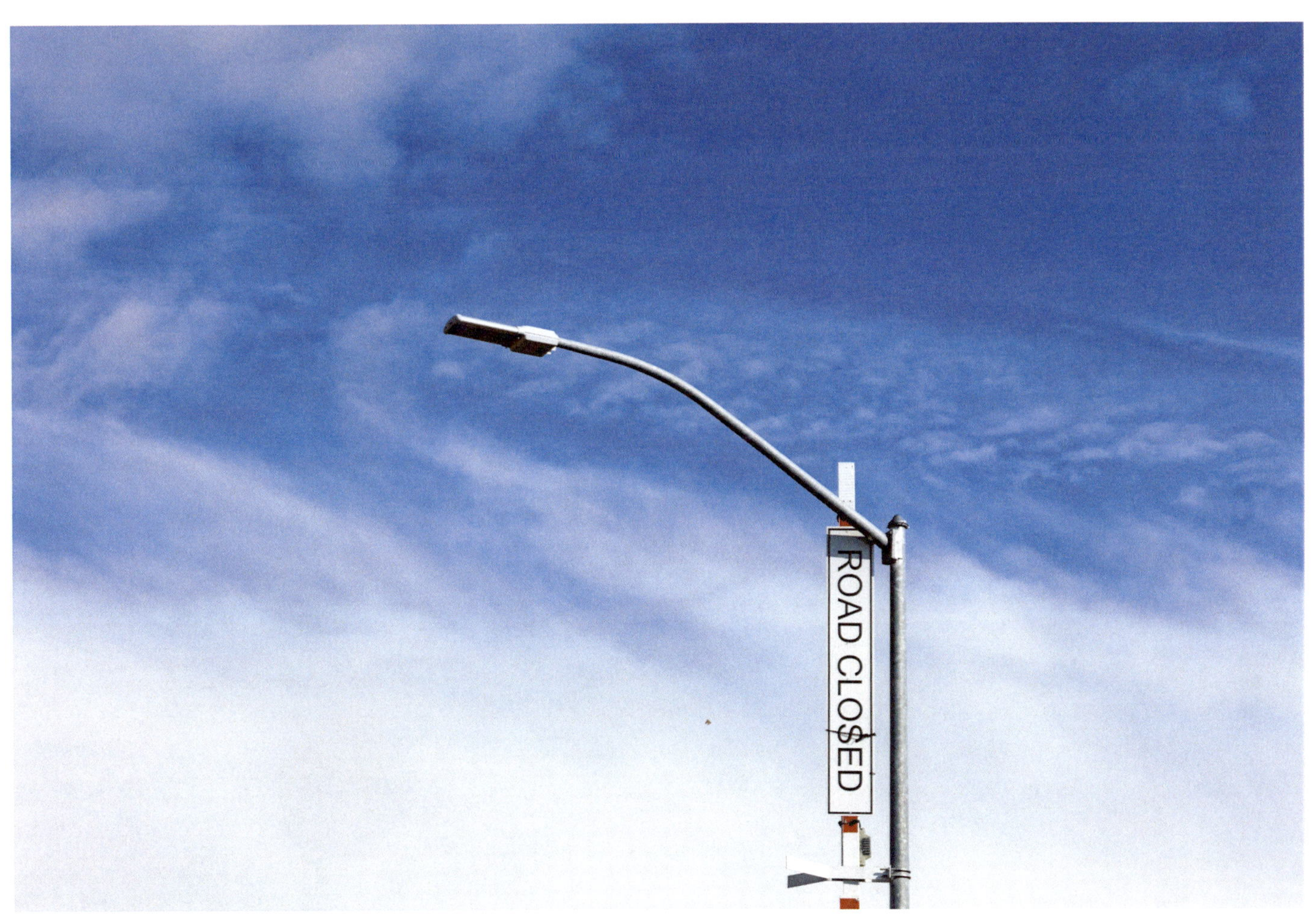
ROAD CLOSED

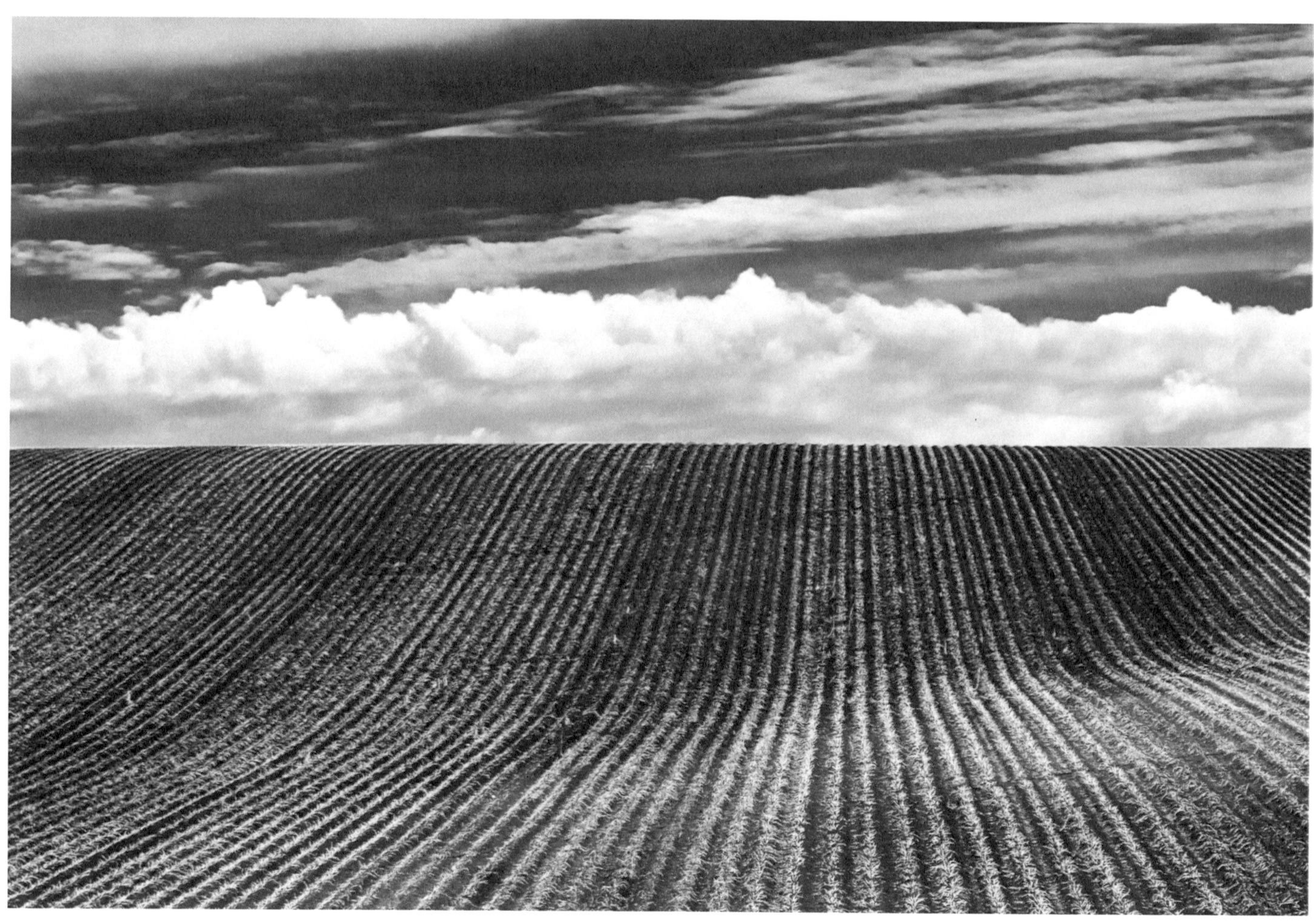

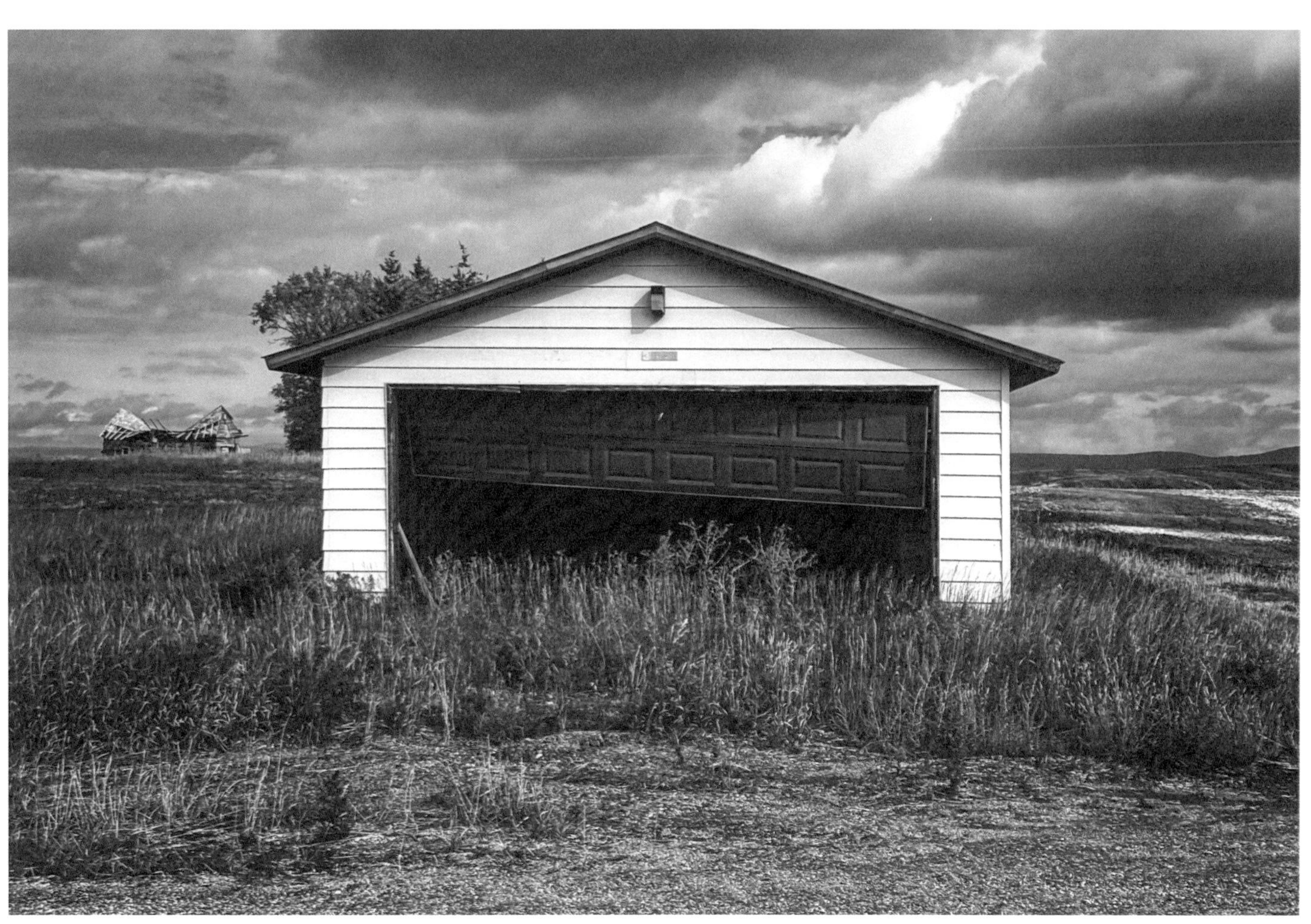

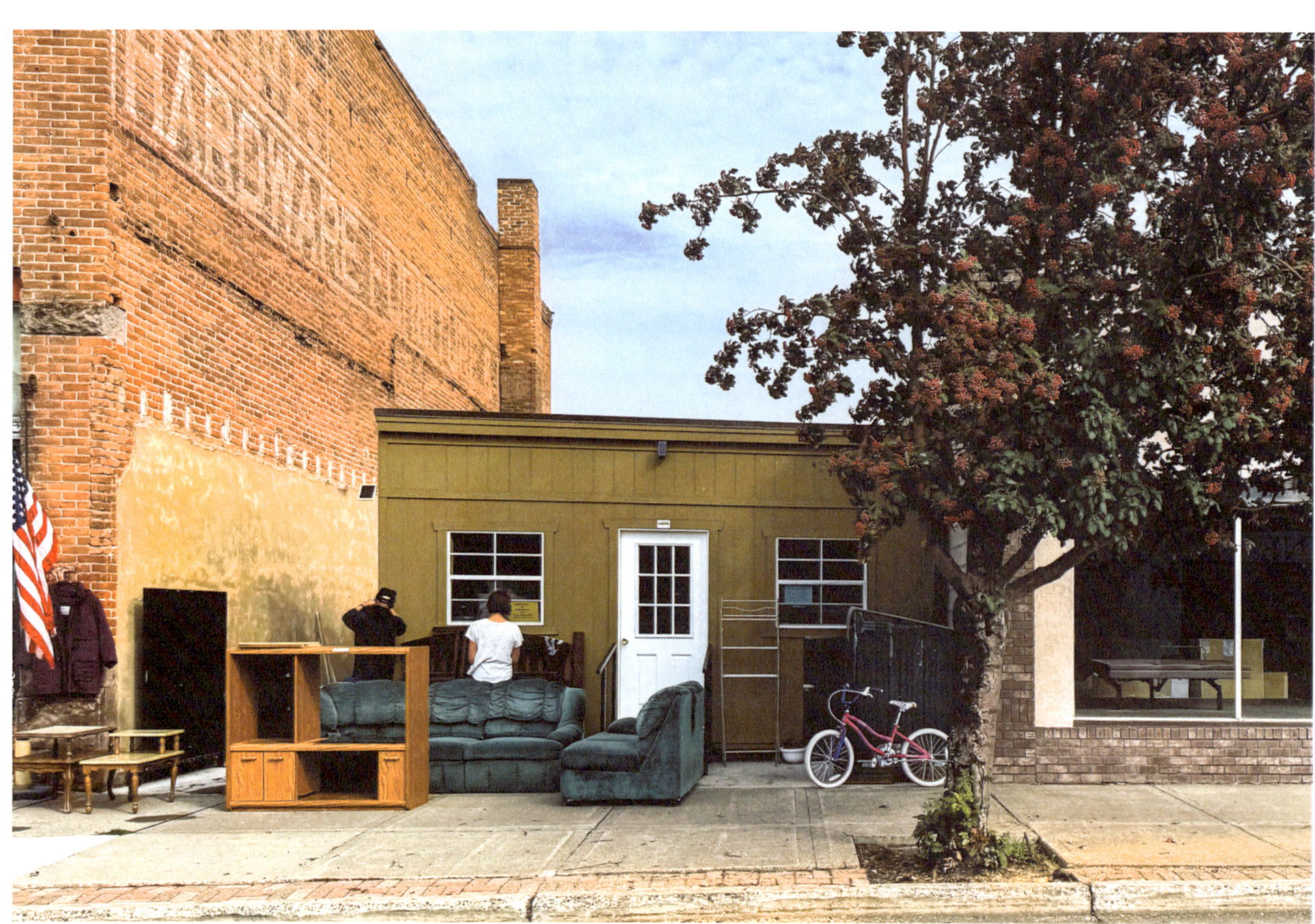

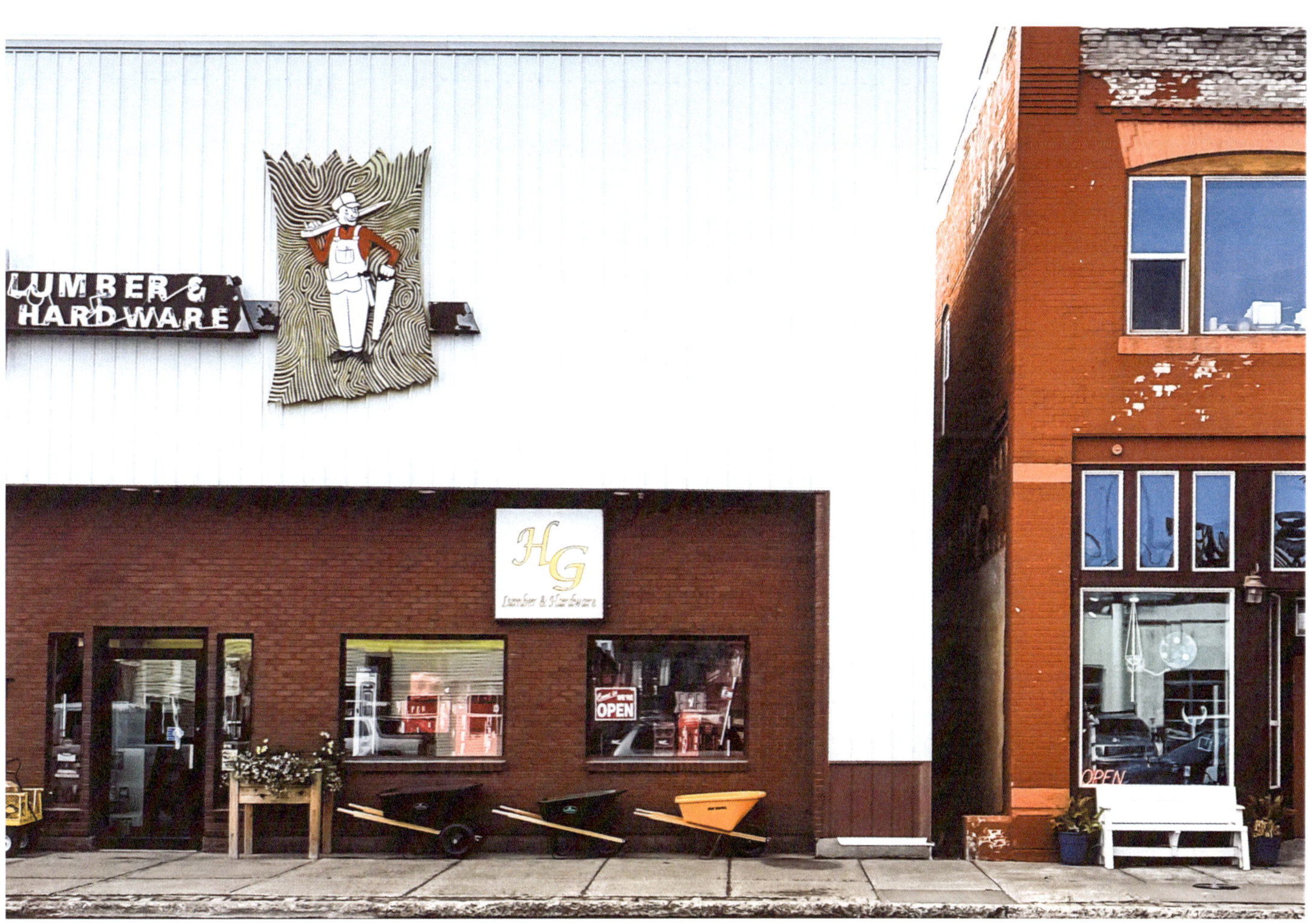

LUMBER &
HARDWARE
HG
OPEN
OPEN

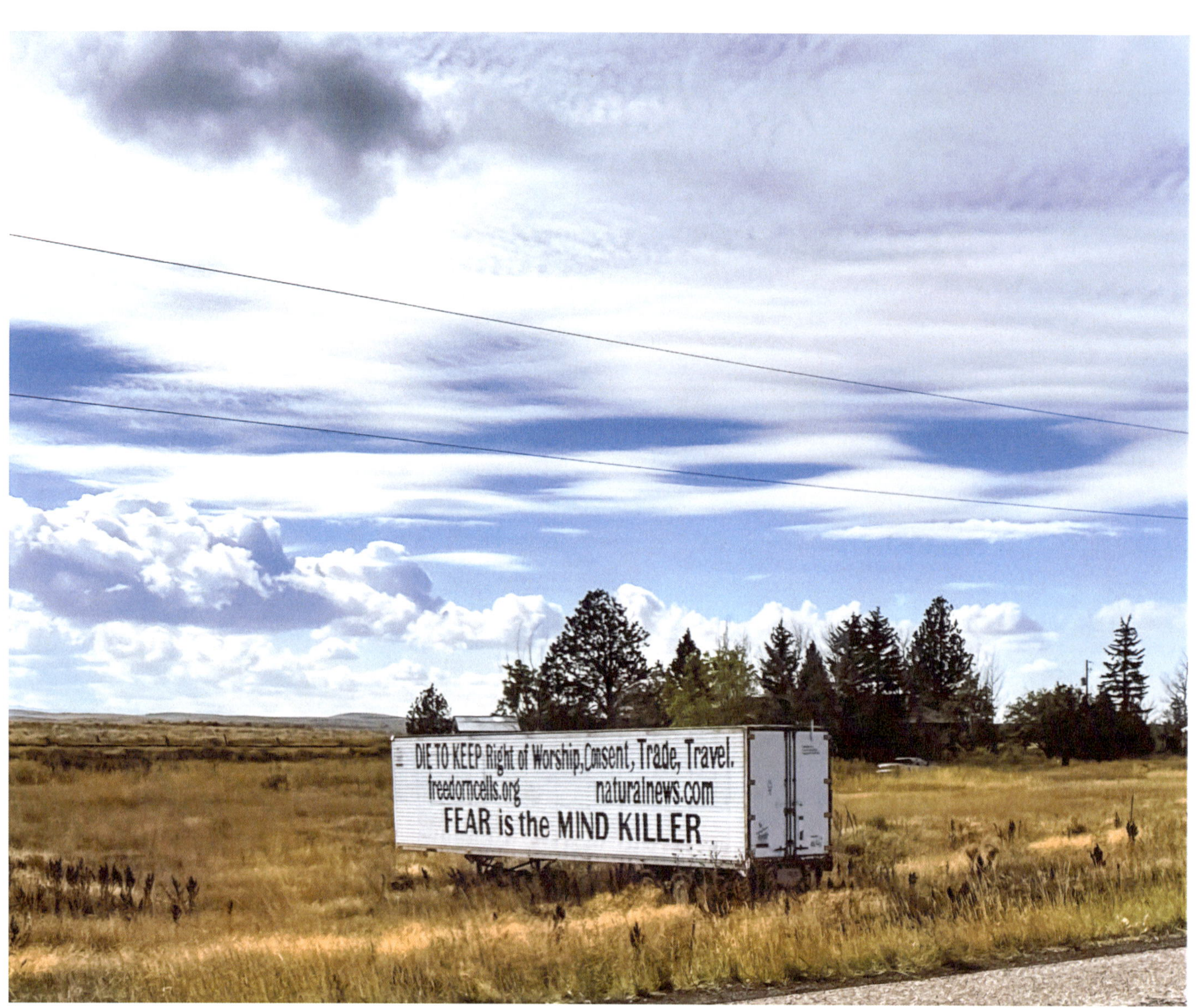

DIE TO KEEP Right of Worship, Consent, Trade, Travel.
freedomcells.org
naturalnews.com
FEAR is the MIND KILLER

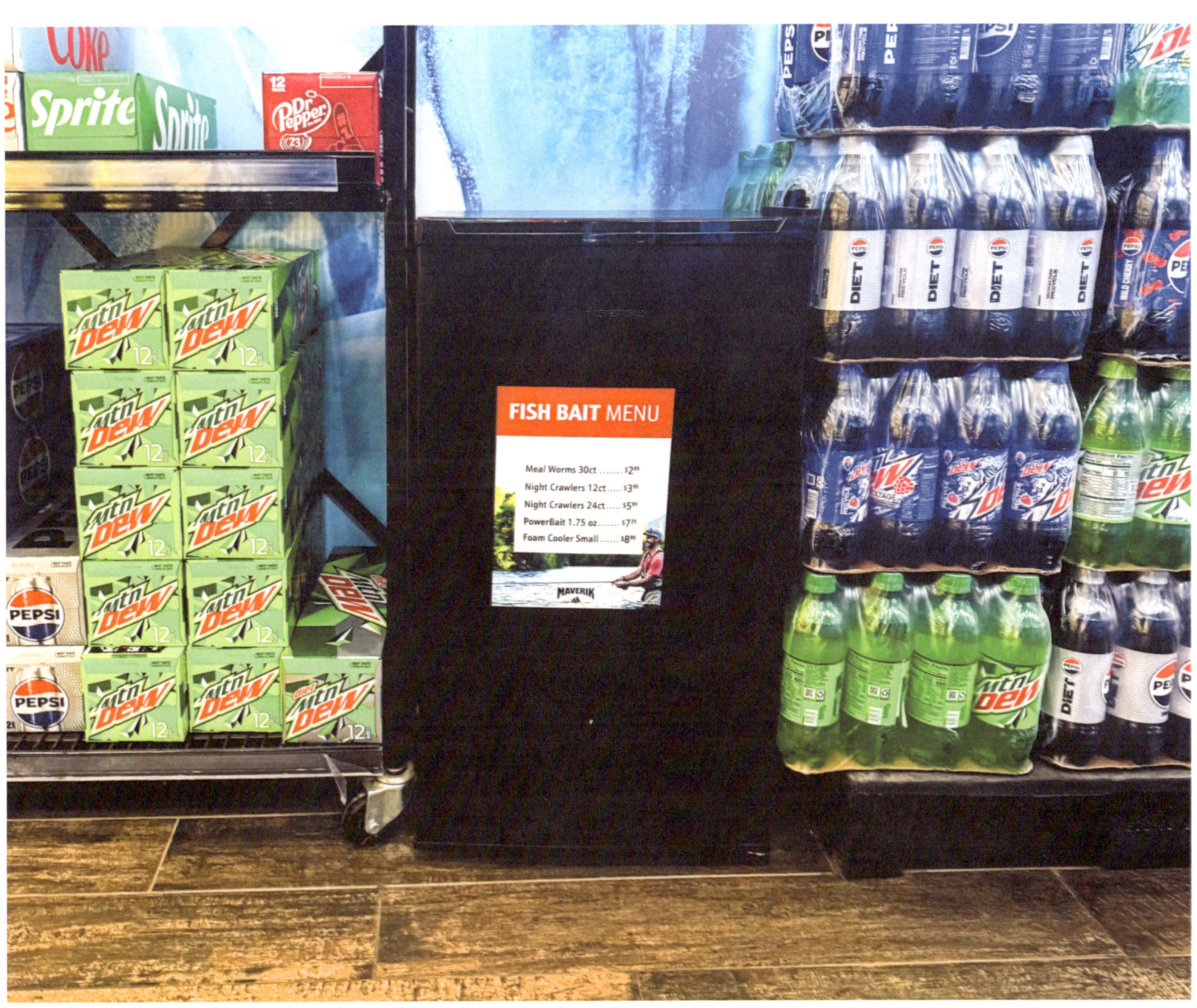
FISH BAIT MENU
Meal Worms 30ct $2.89
Night Crawlers 12ct $3.99
Night Crawlers 24ct $5.99
PowerBait 1.75 oz $7.25
Foam Cooler Small $8.99
MAVERIK

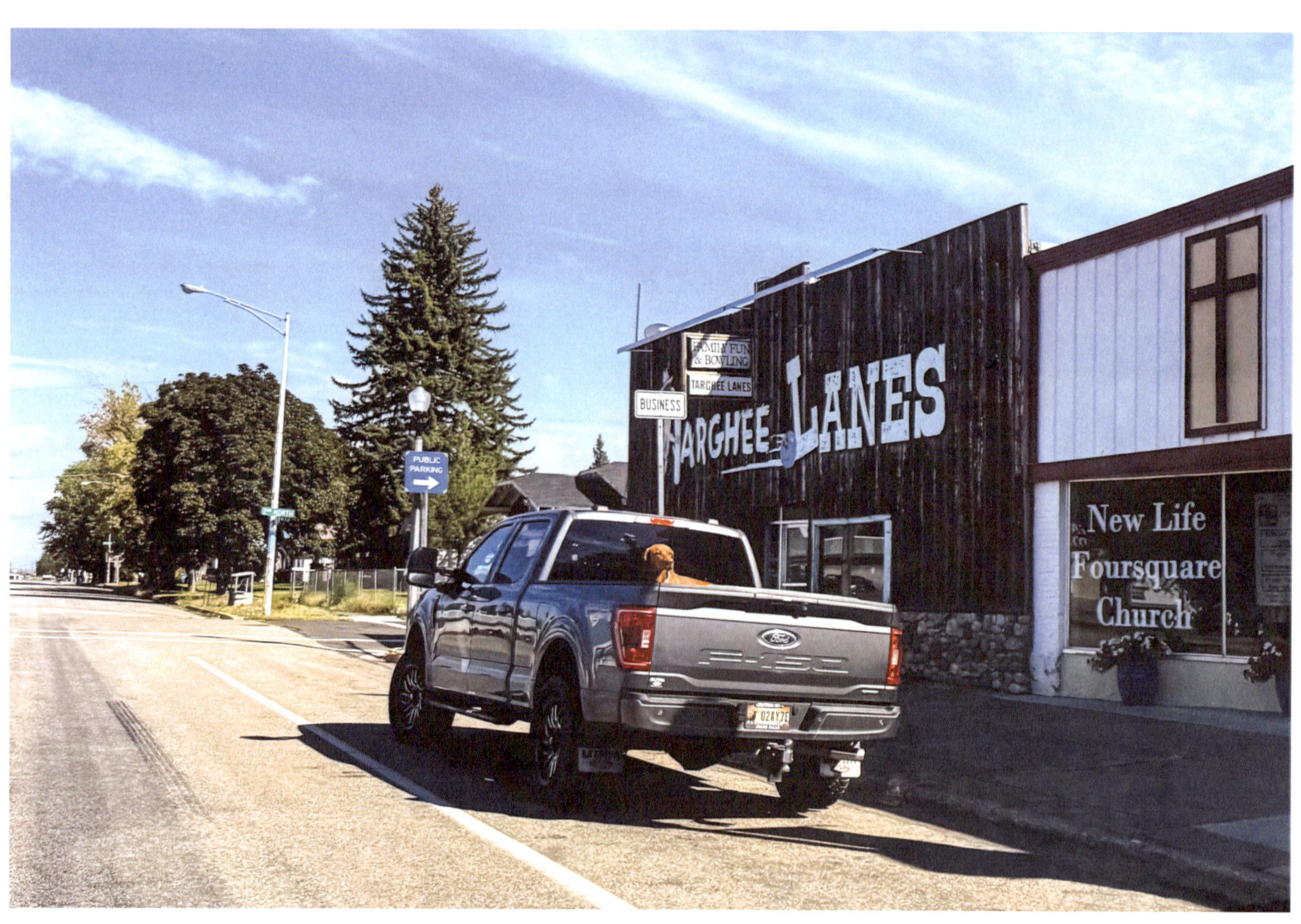
FAMILY FUN & BOWLING
TARGHEE LANES
BUSINESS
TARGHEE LANES
PUBLIC PARKING
NORTH
New Life
Foursquare
Church
Ford
F-150

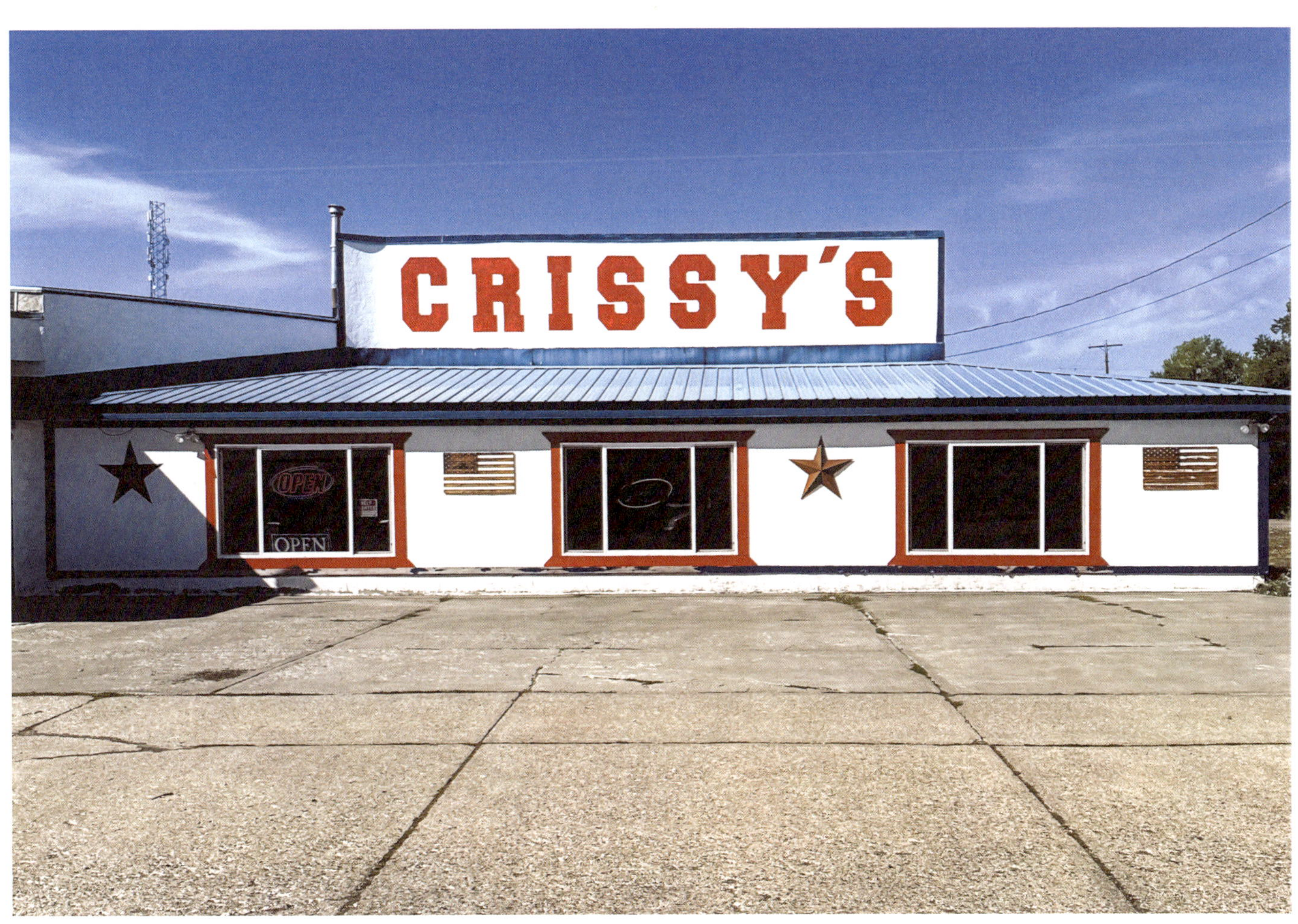

CRISSY'S
OPEN
OPEN

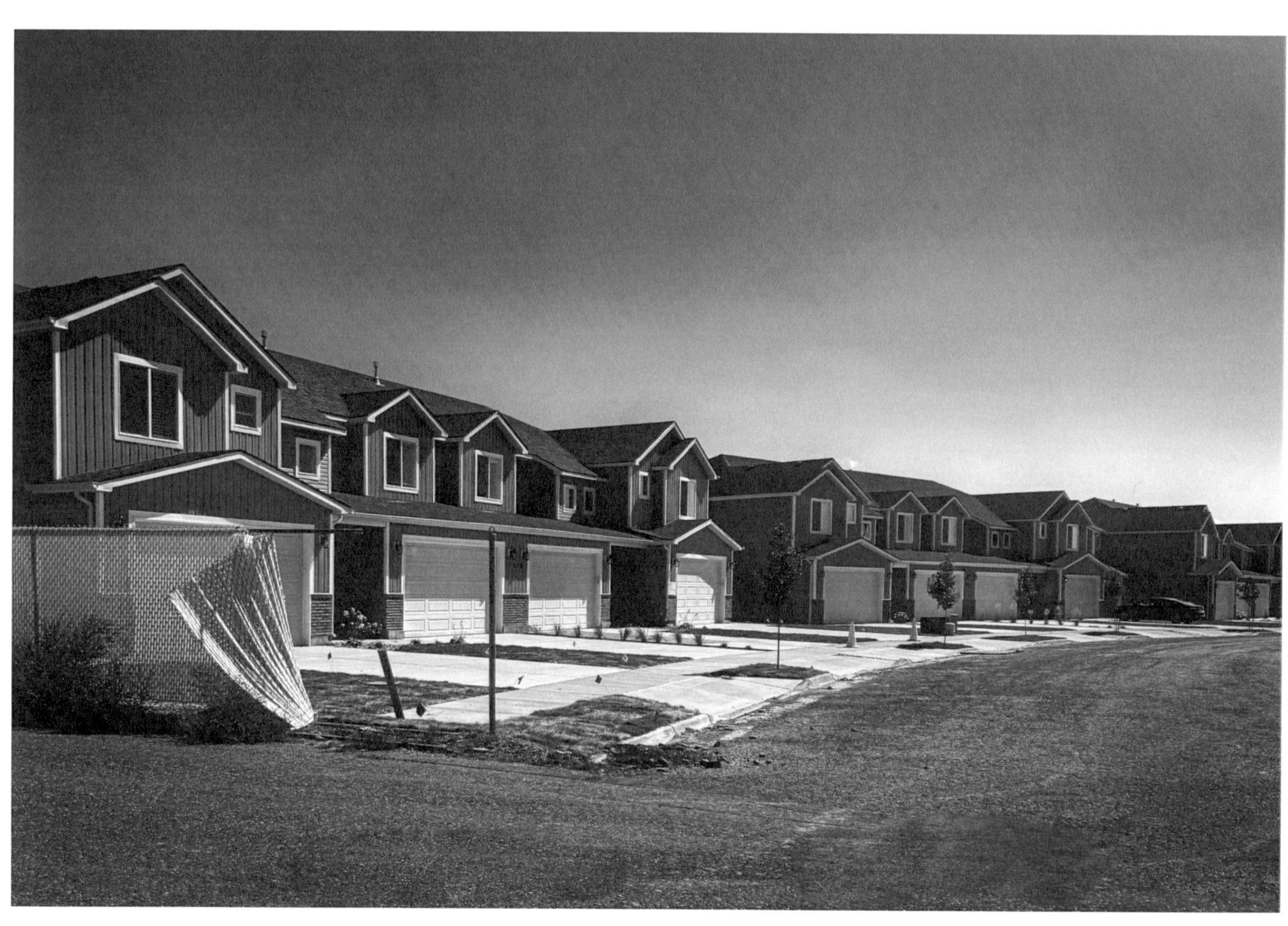

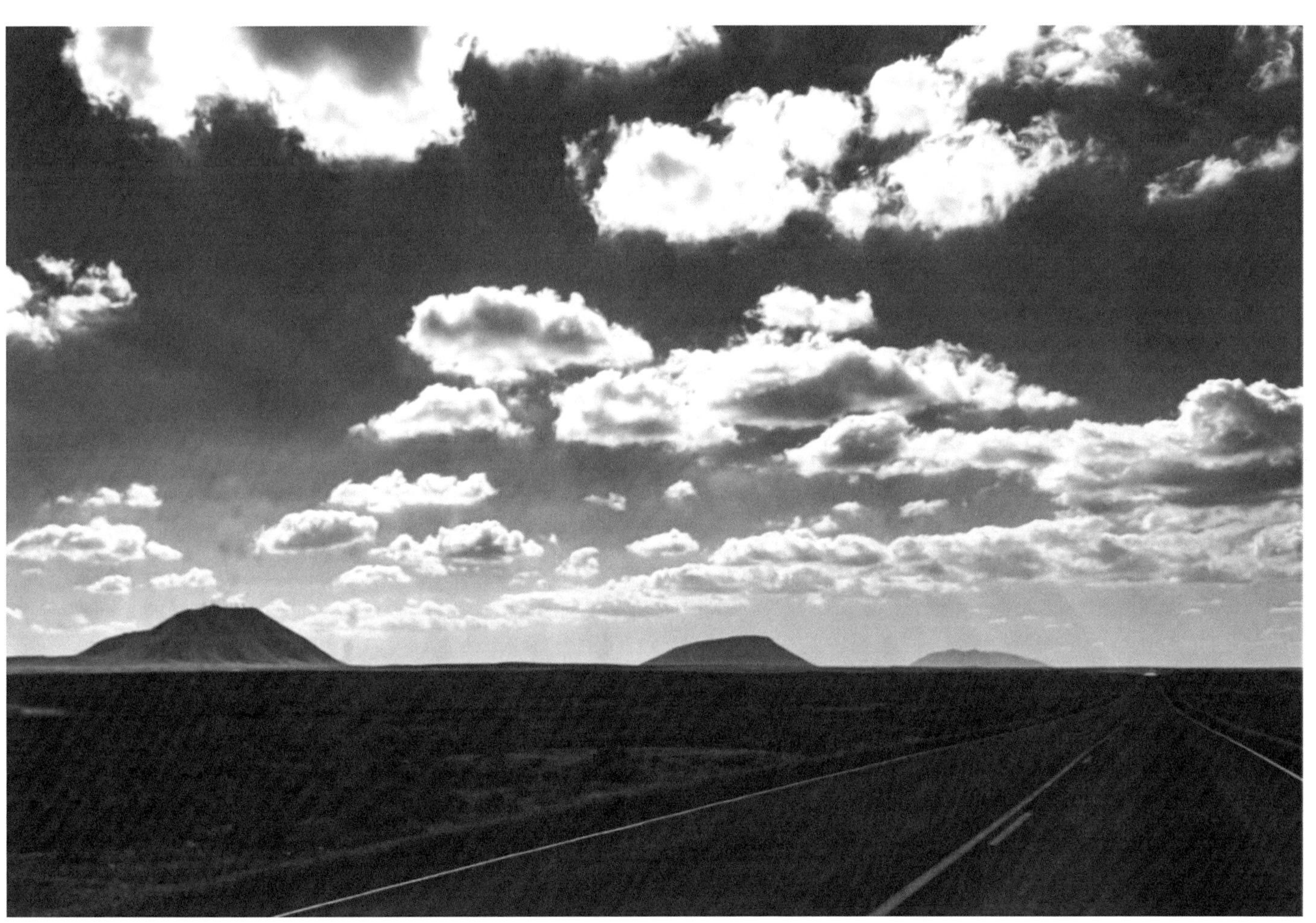

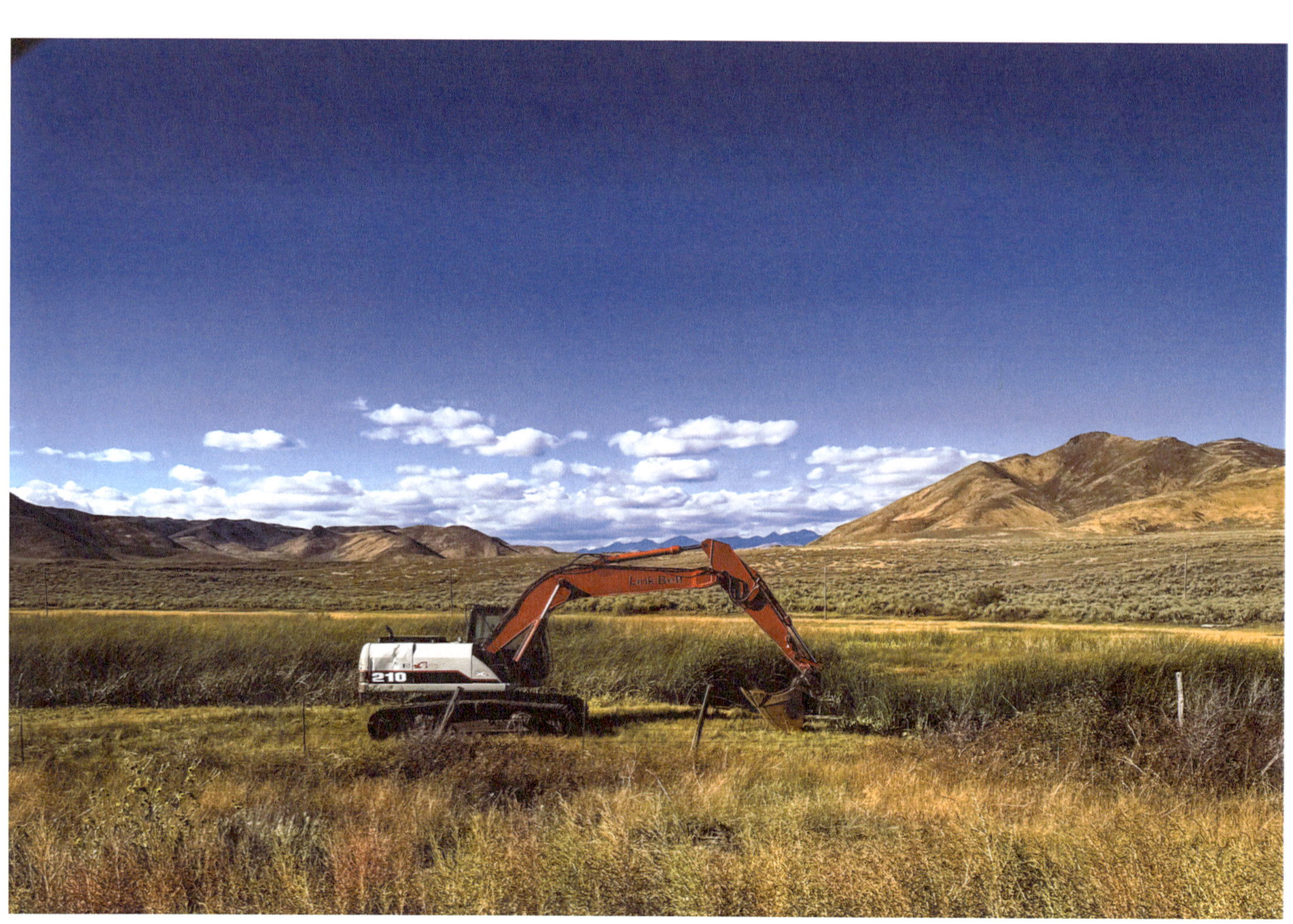

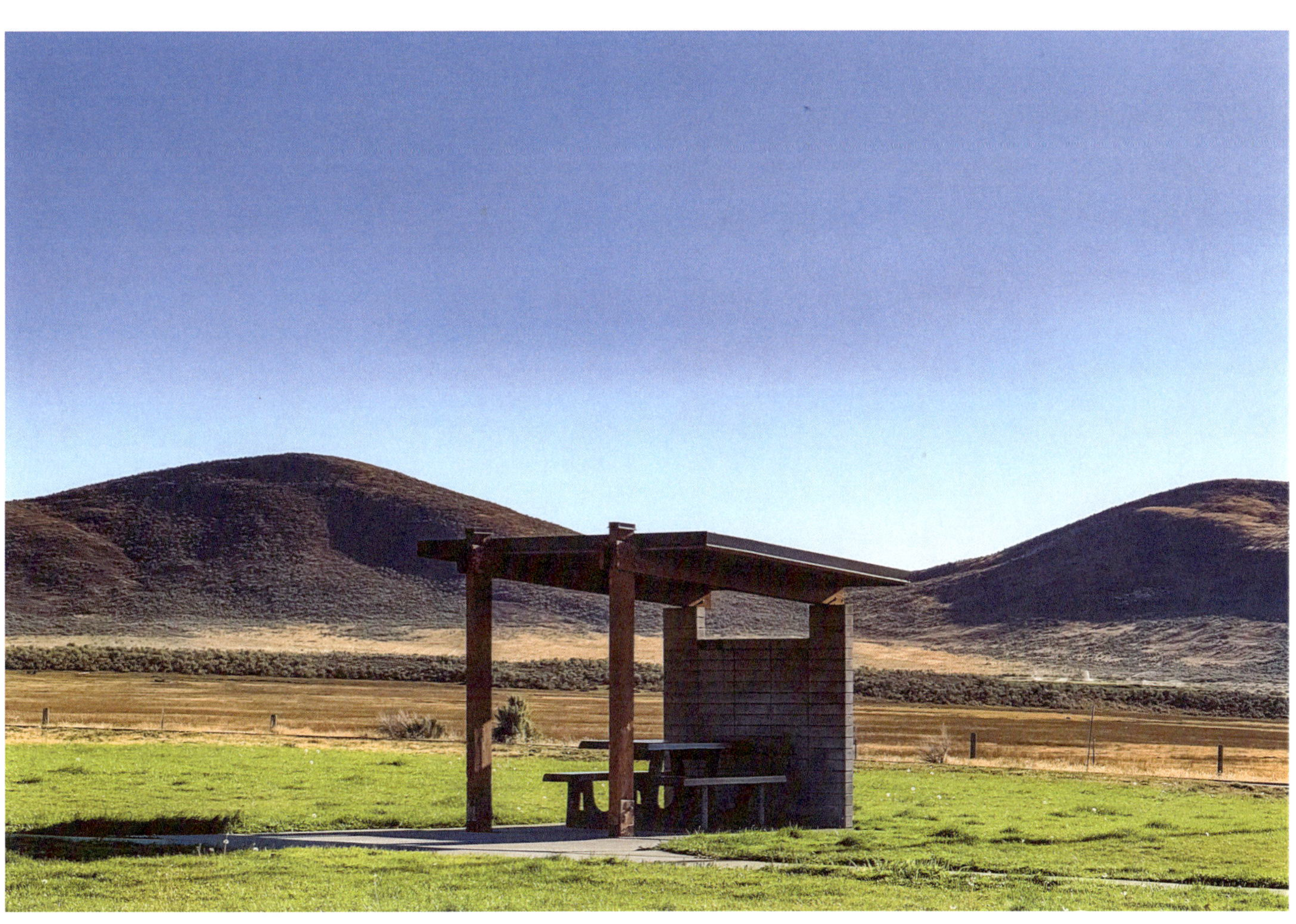

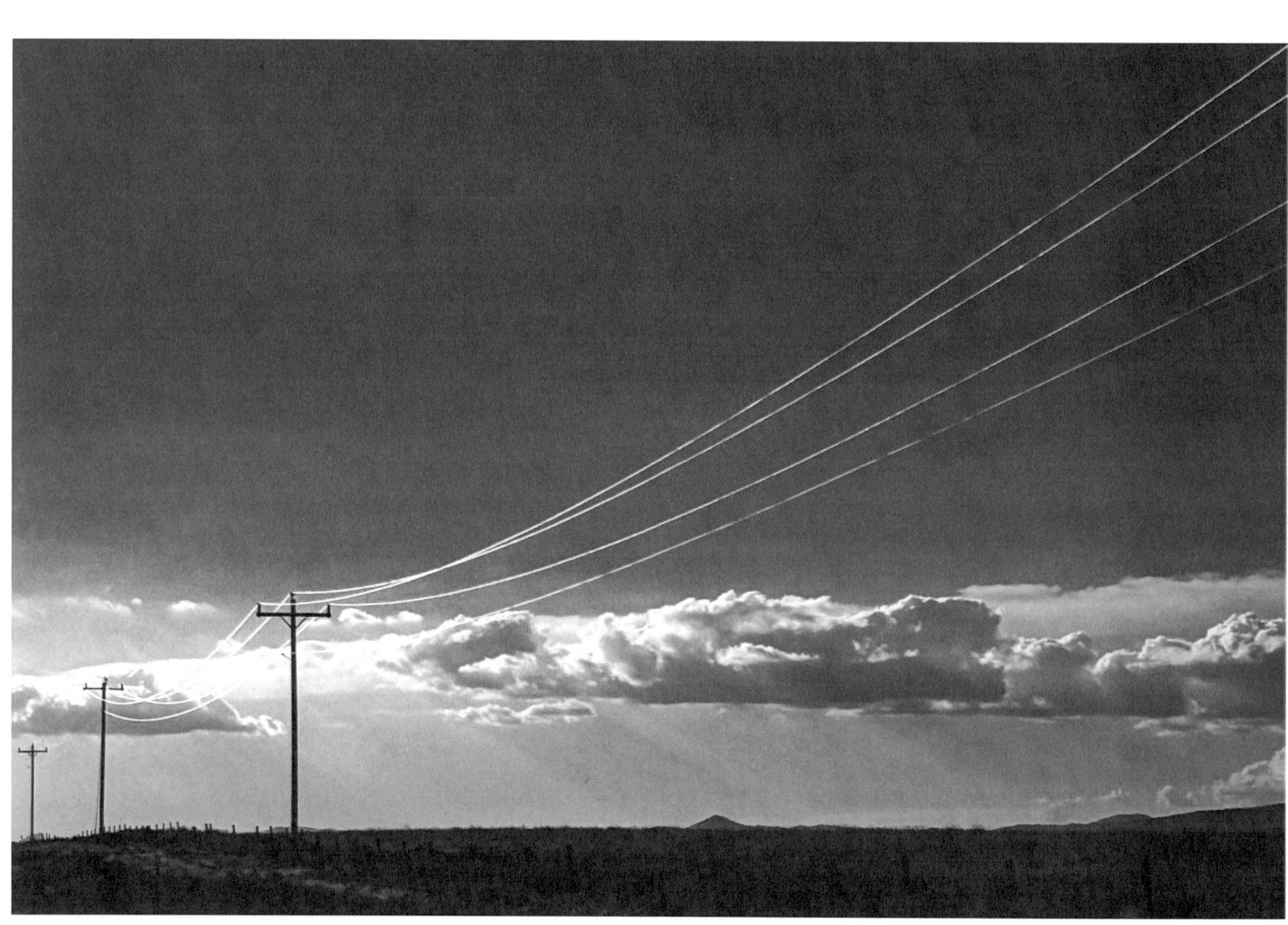

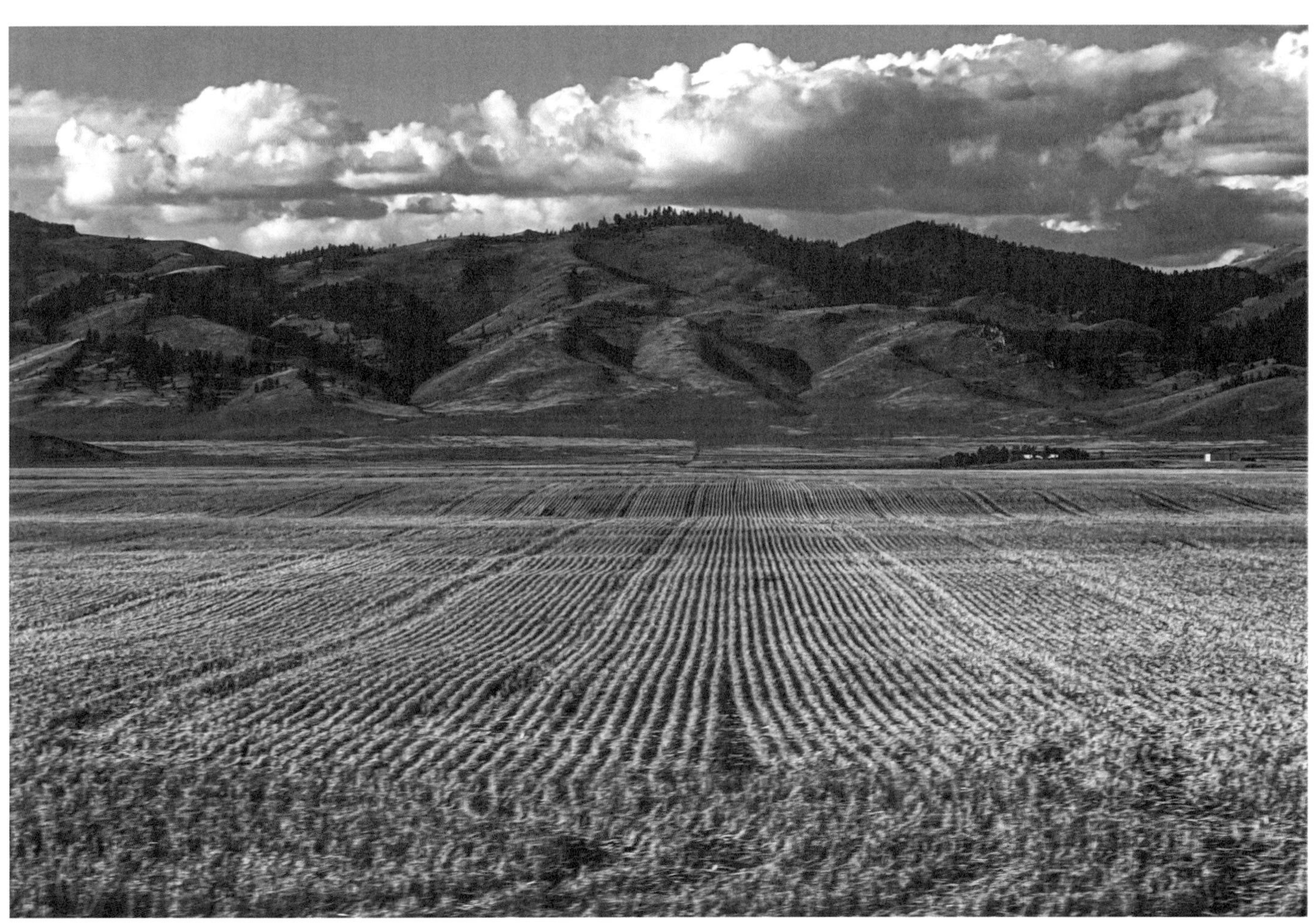

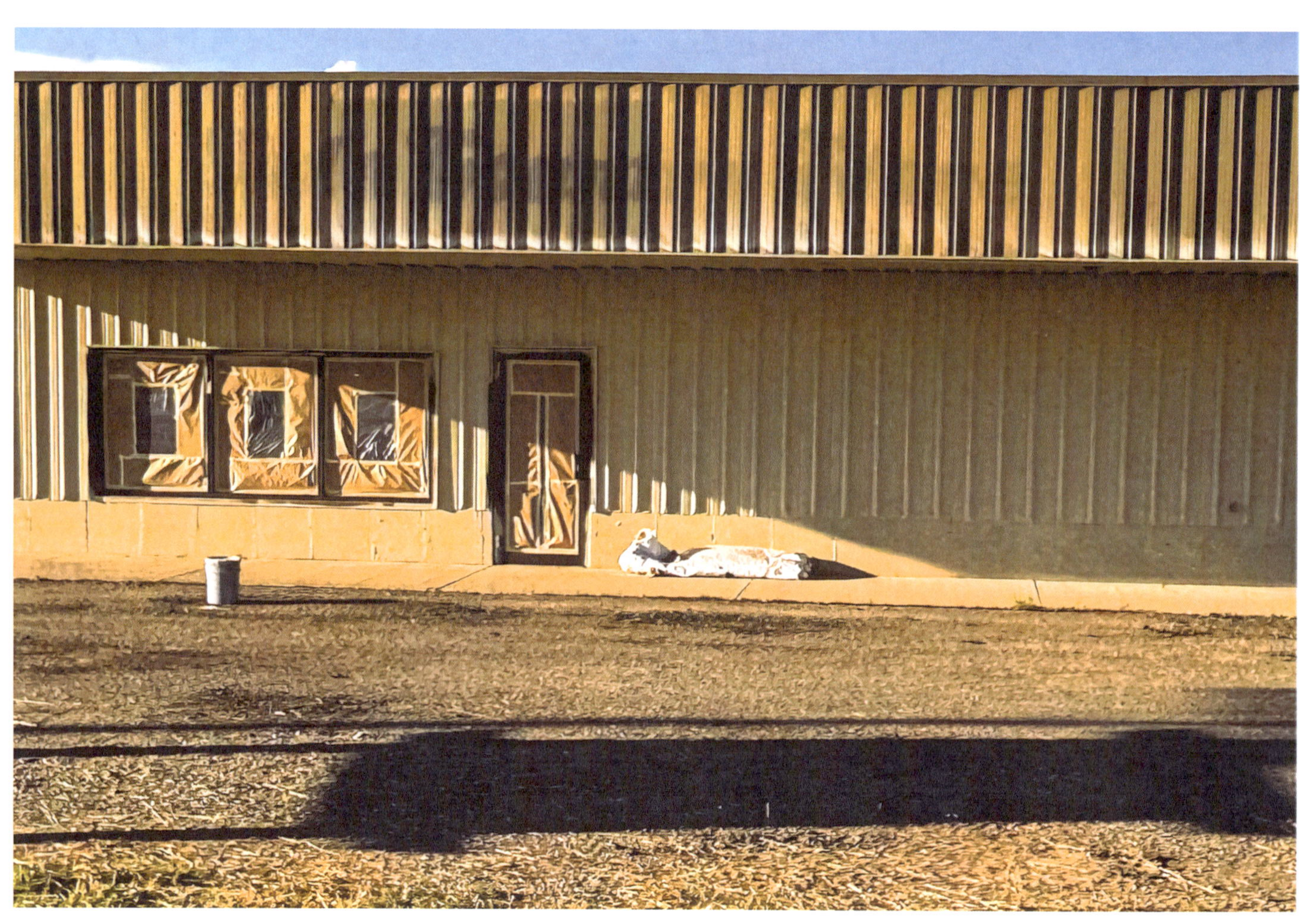

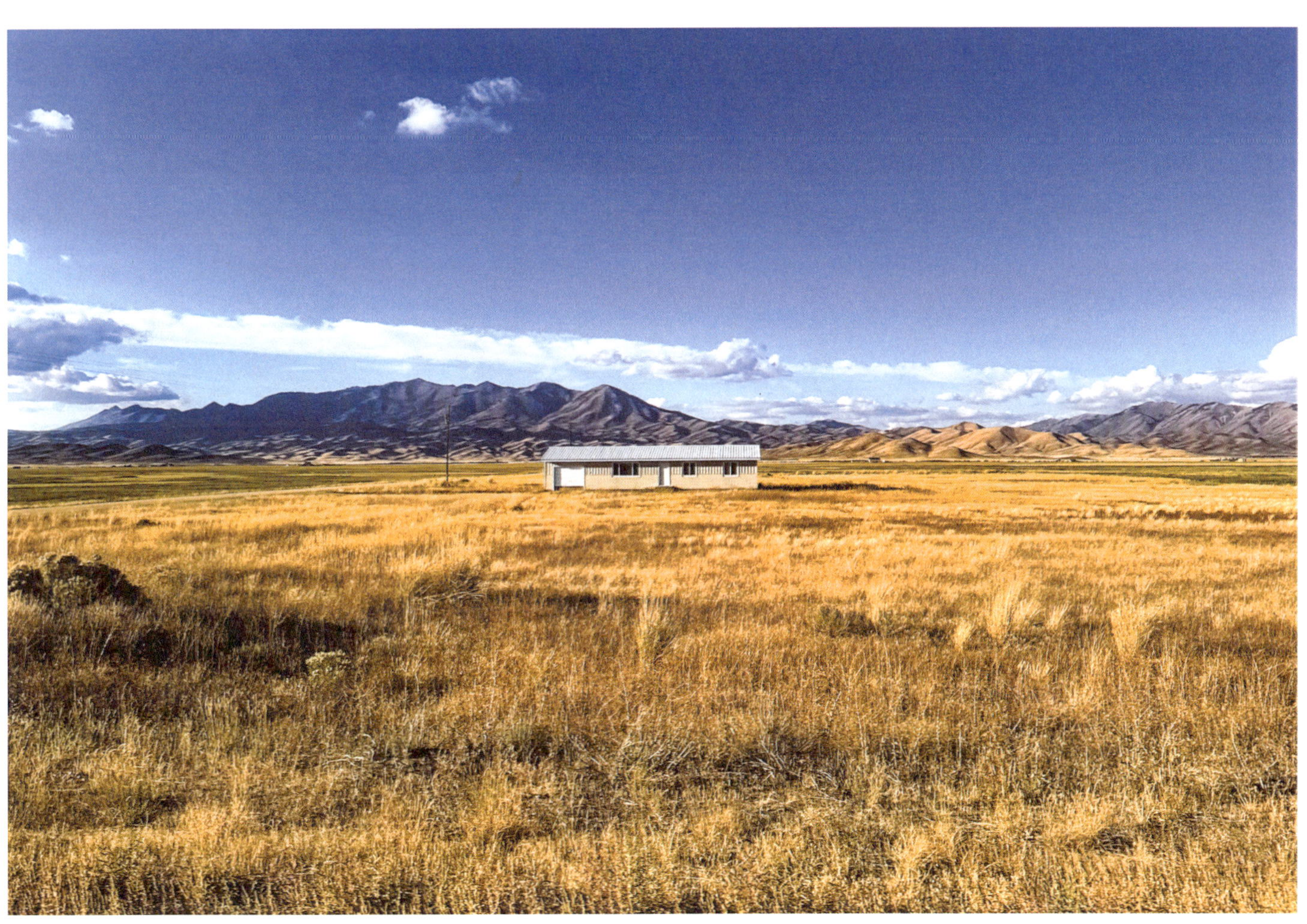

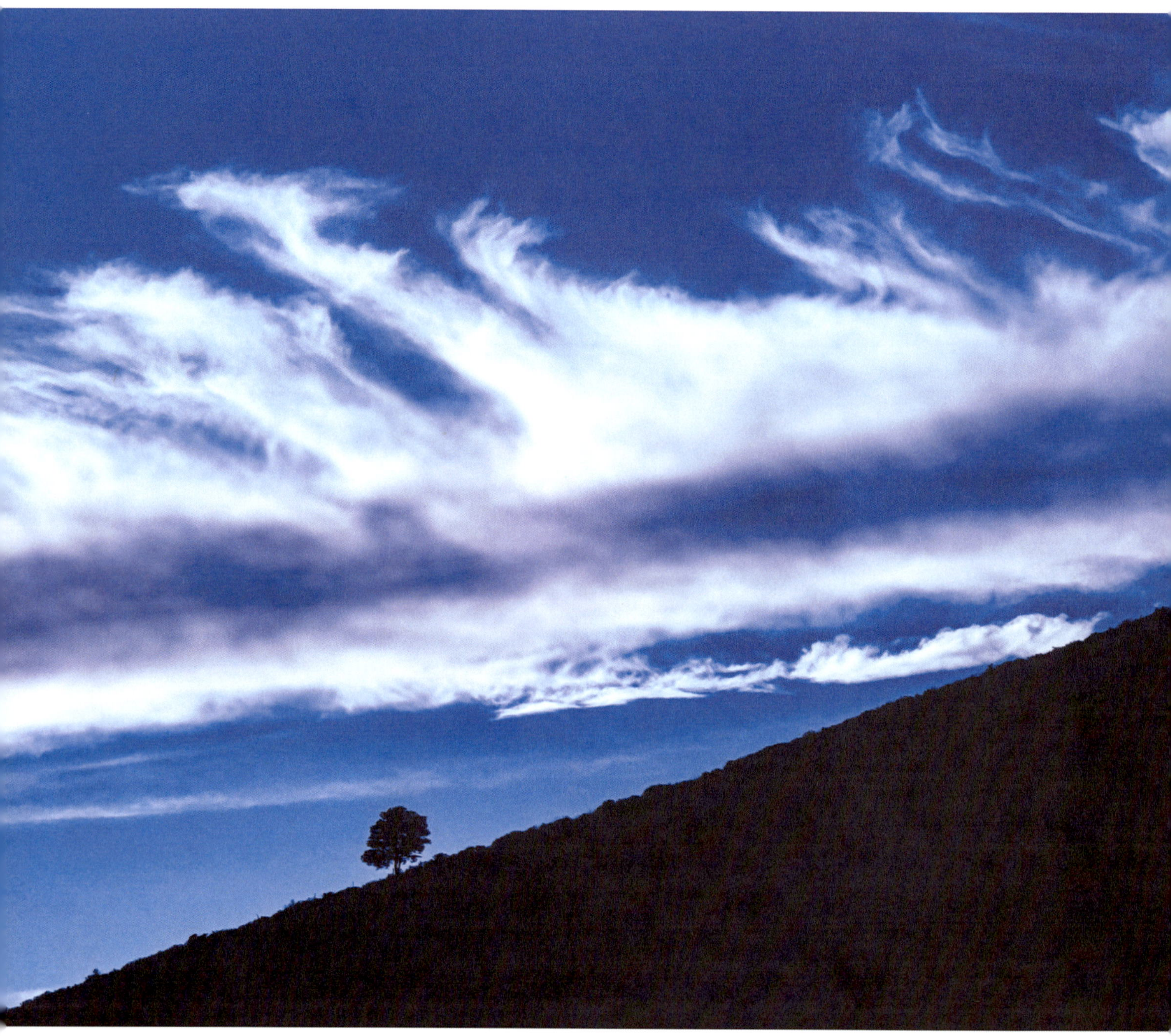

79,000 Steps

Walks in New York City
(mostly mid to lower Manhattan)
during August 2022.

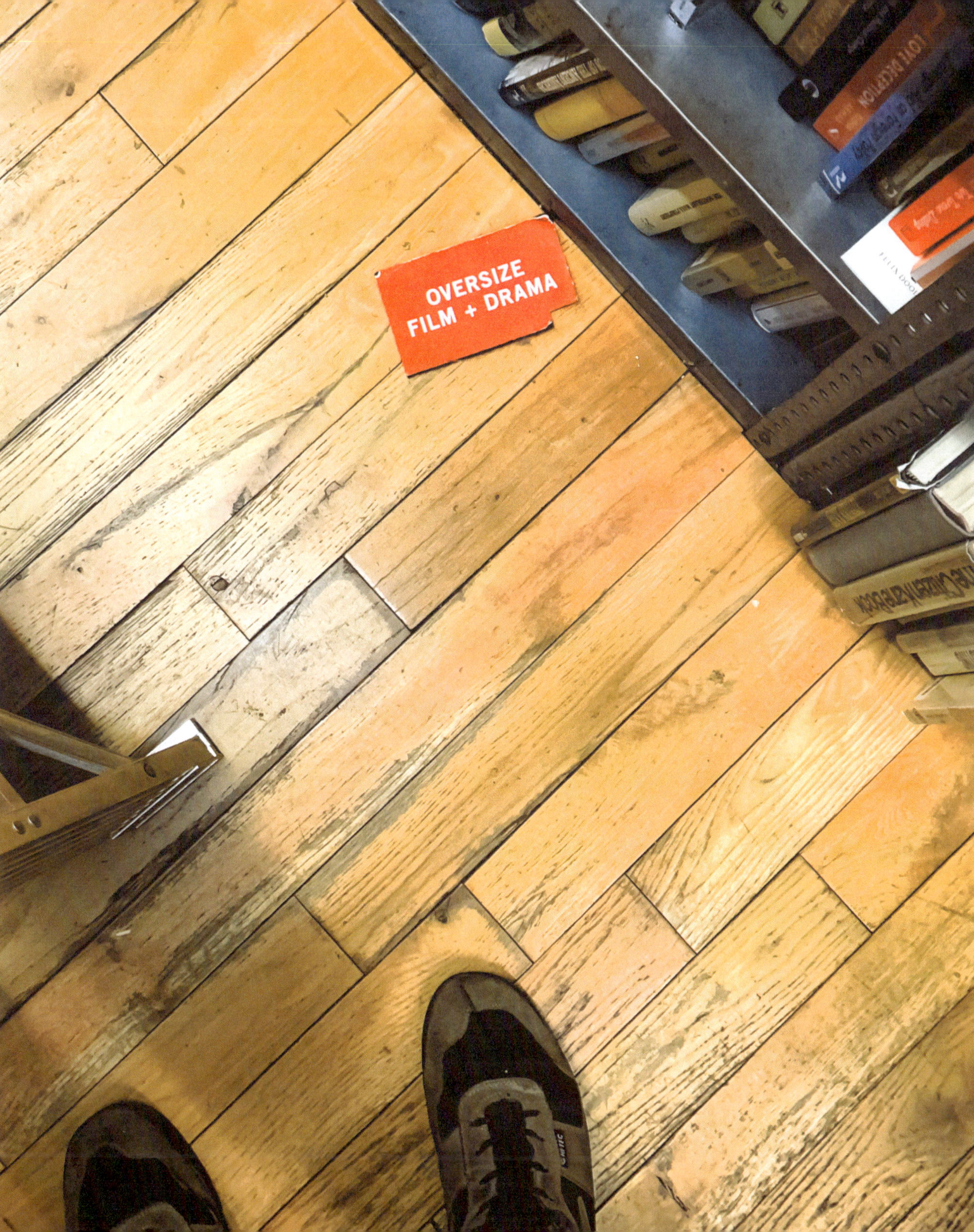
OVERSIZE
FILM + DRAMA

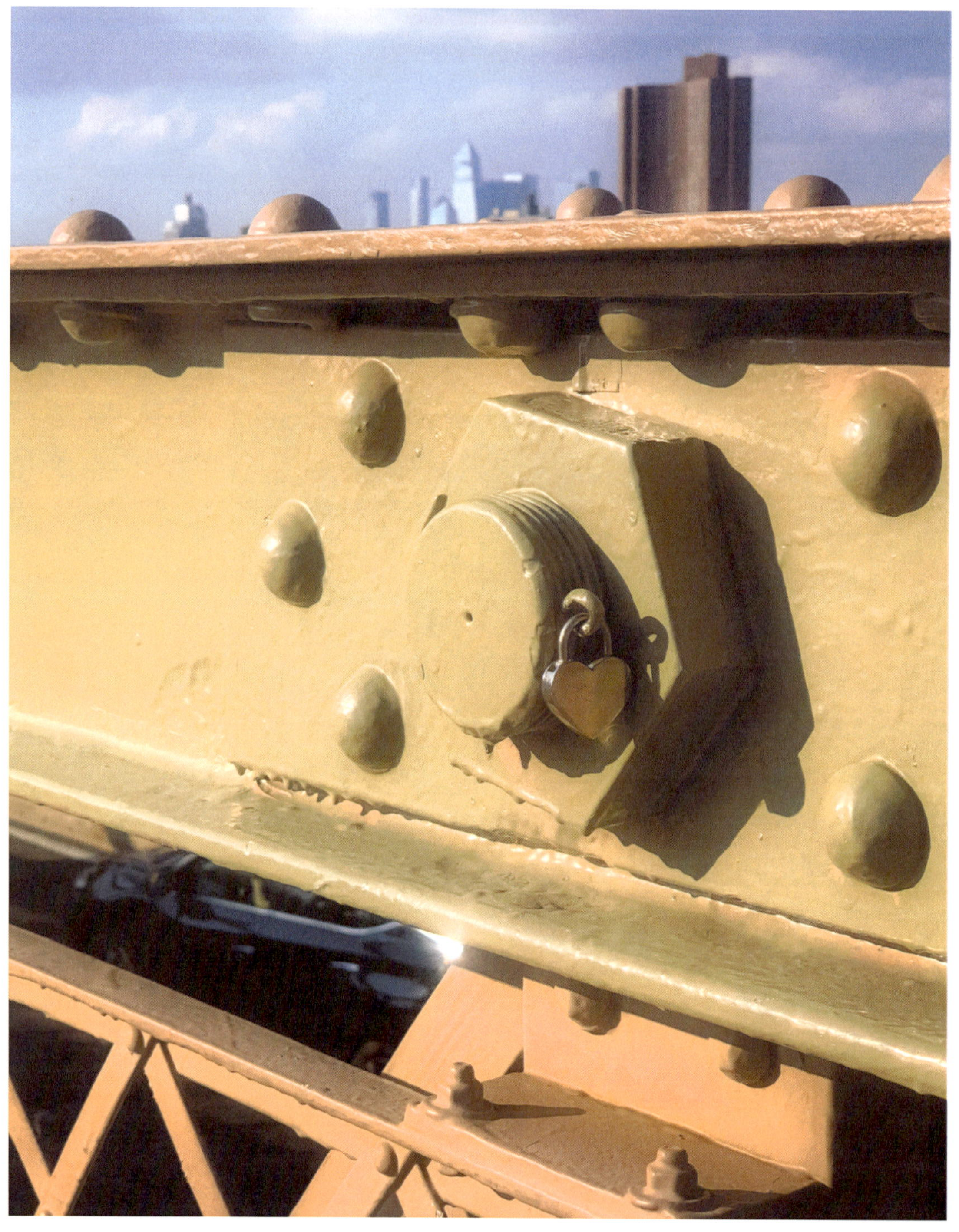

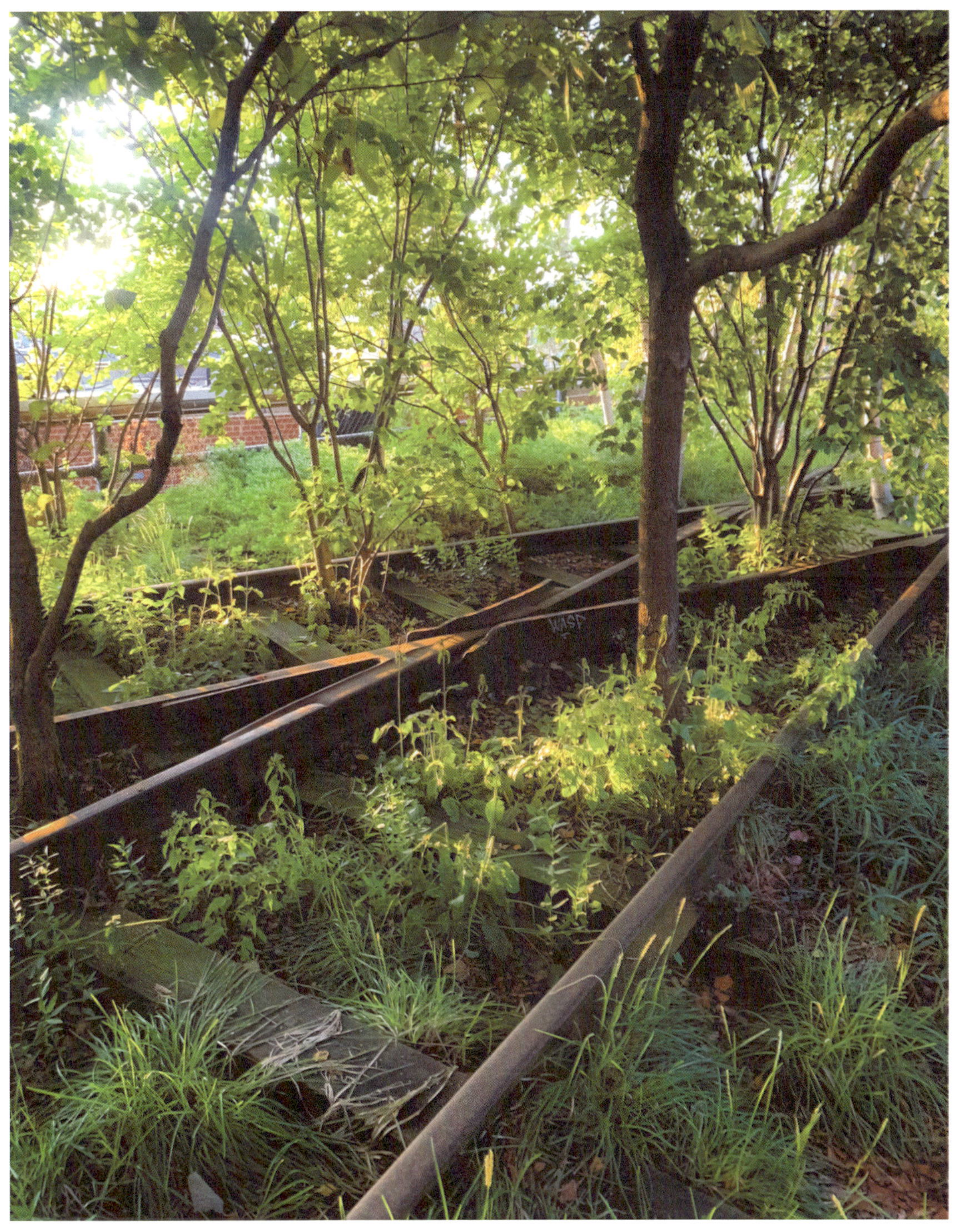

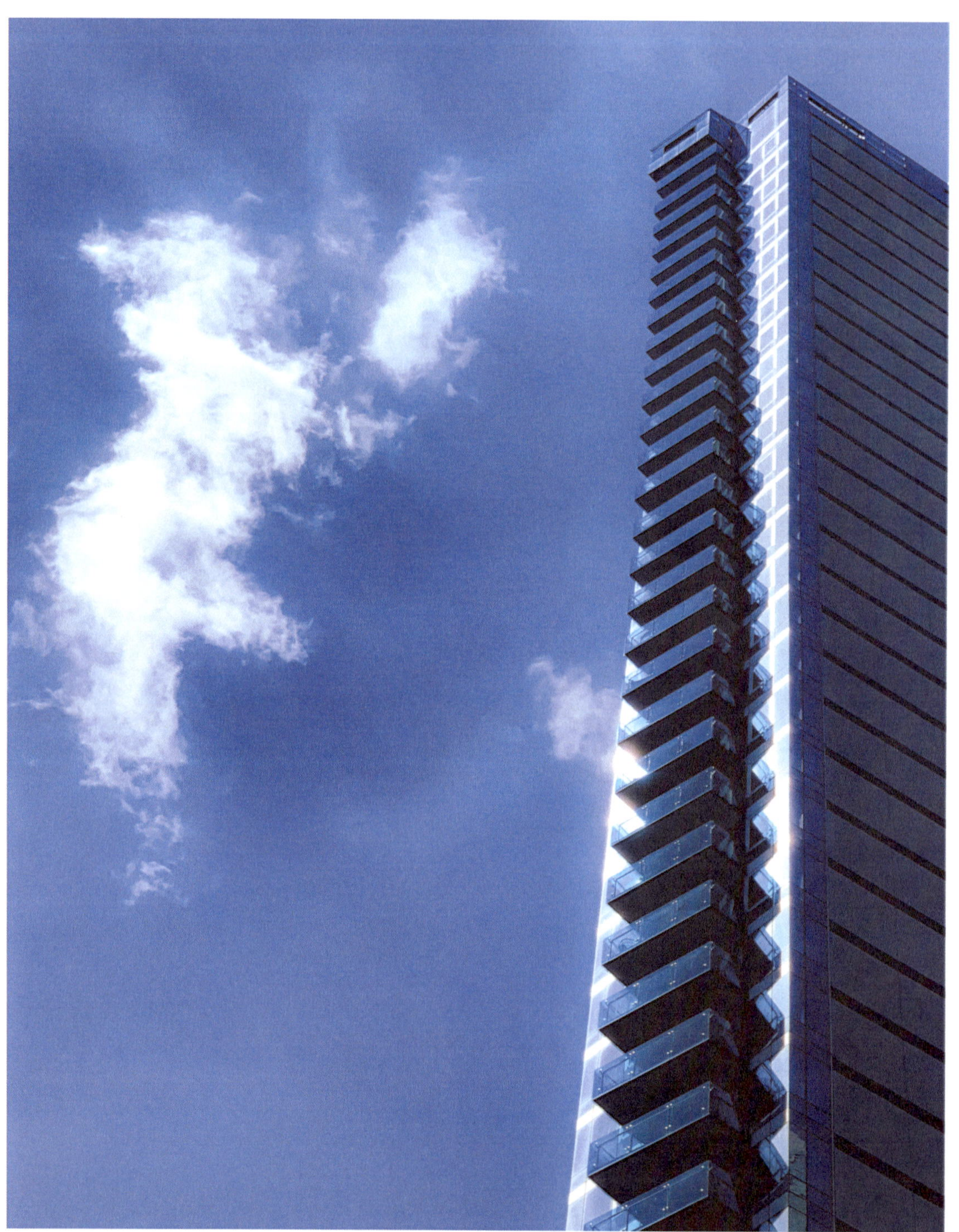

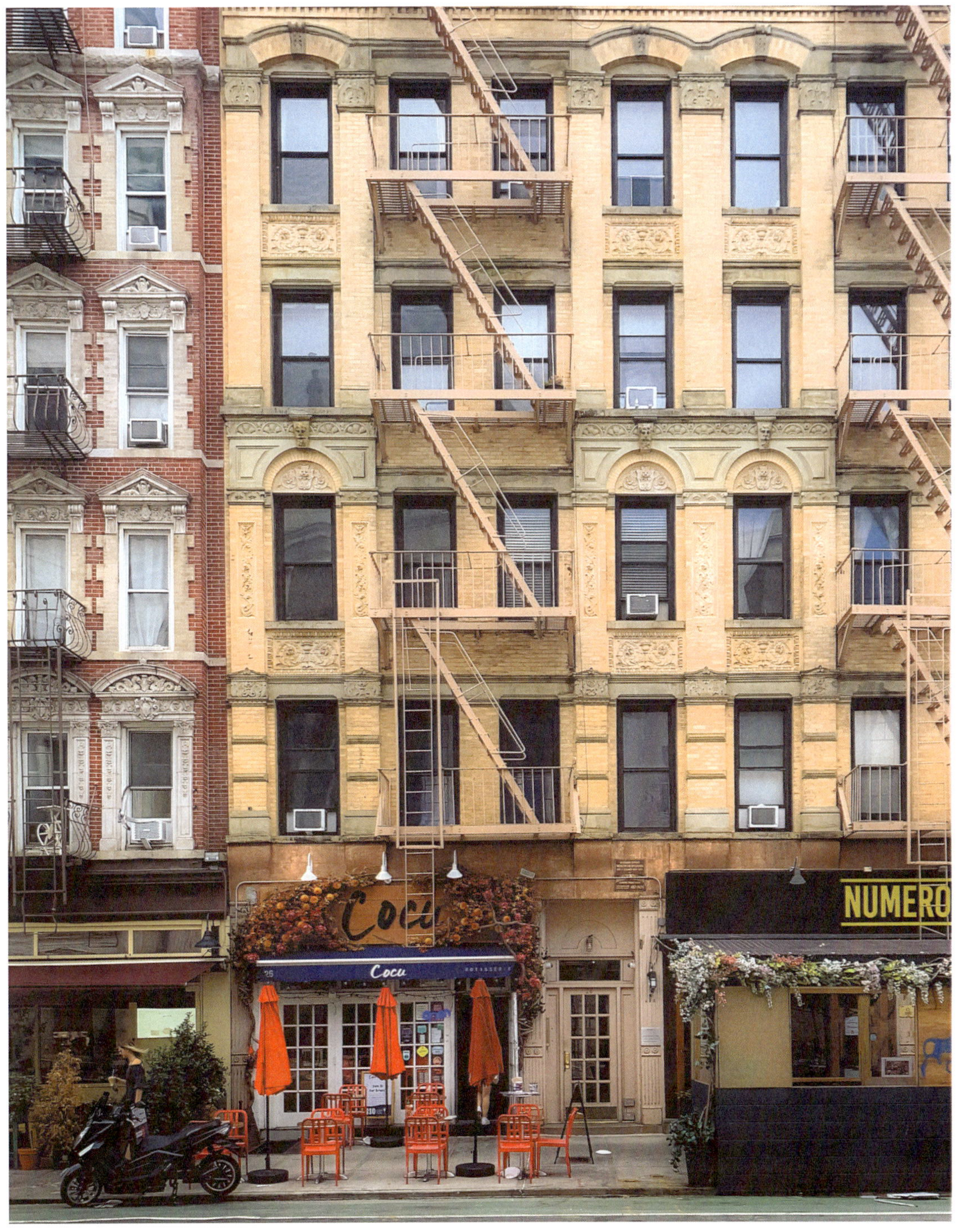
Cocu
Cocu
NUMERO

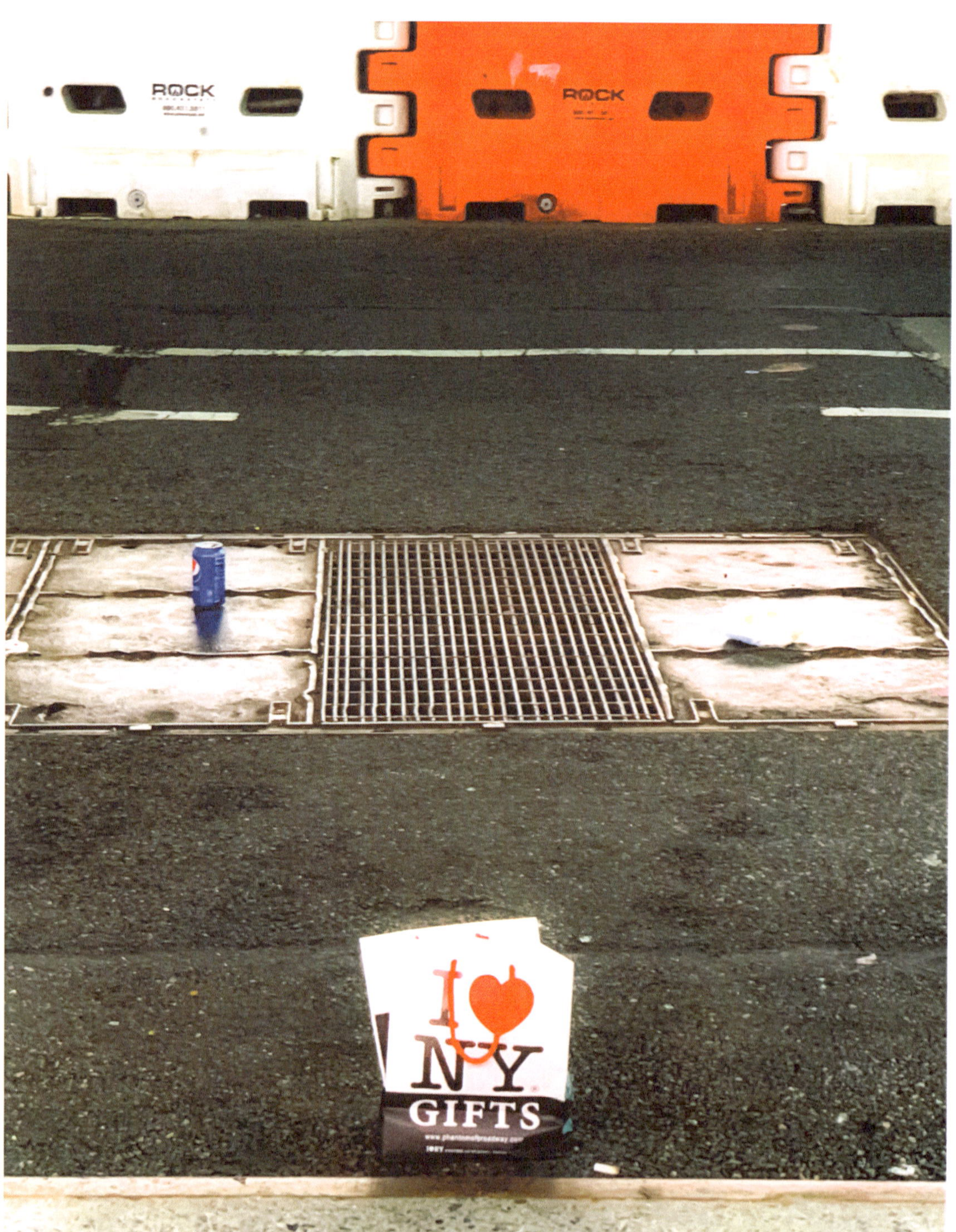
ROCK
ROCK
I ♥ NY
GIFTS

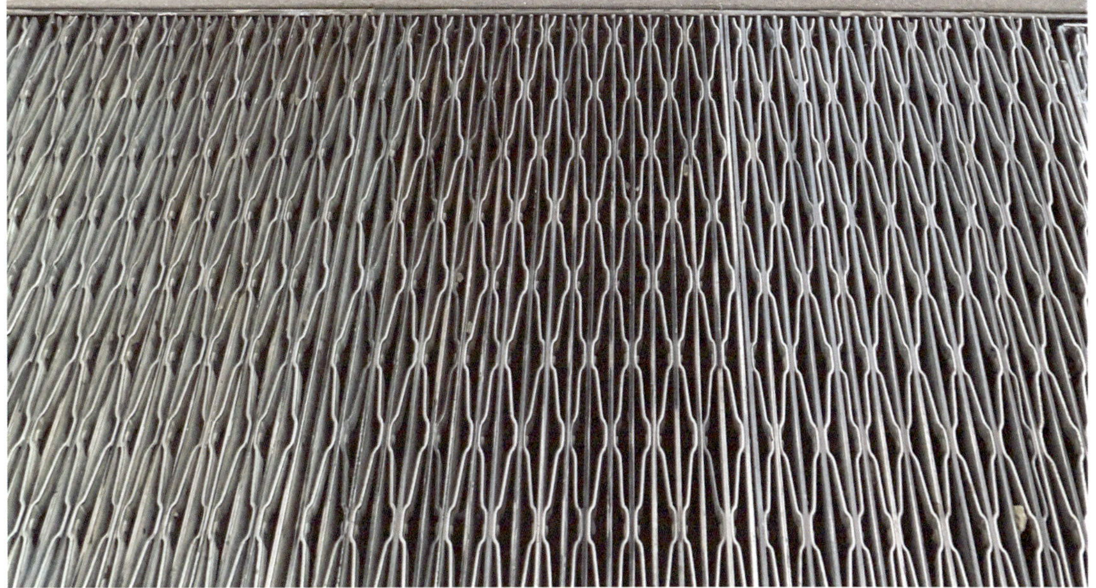

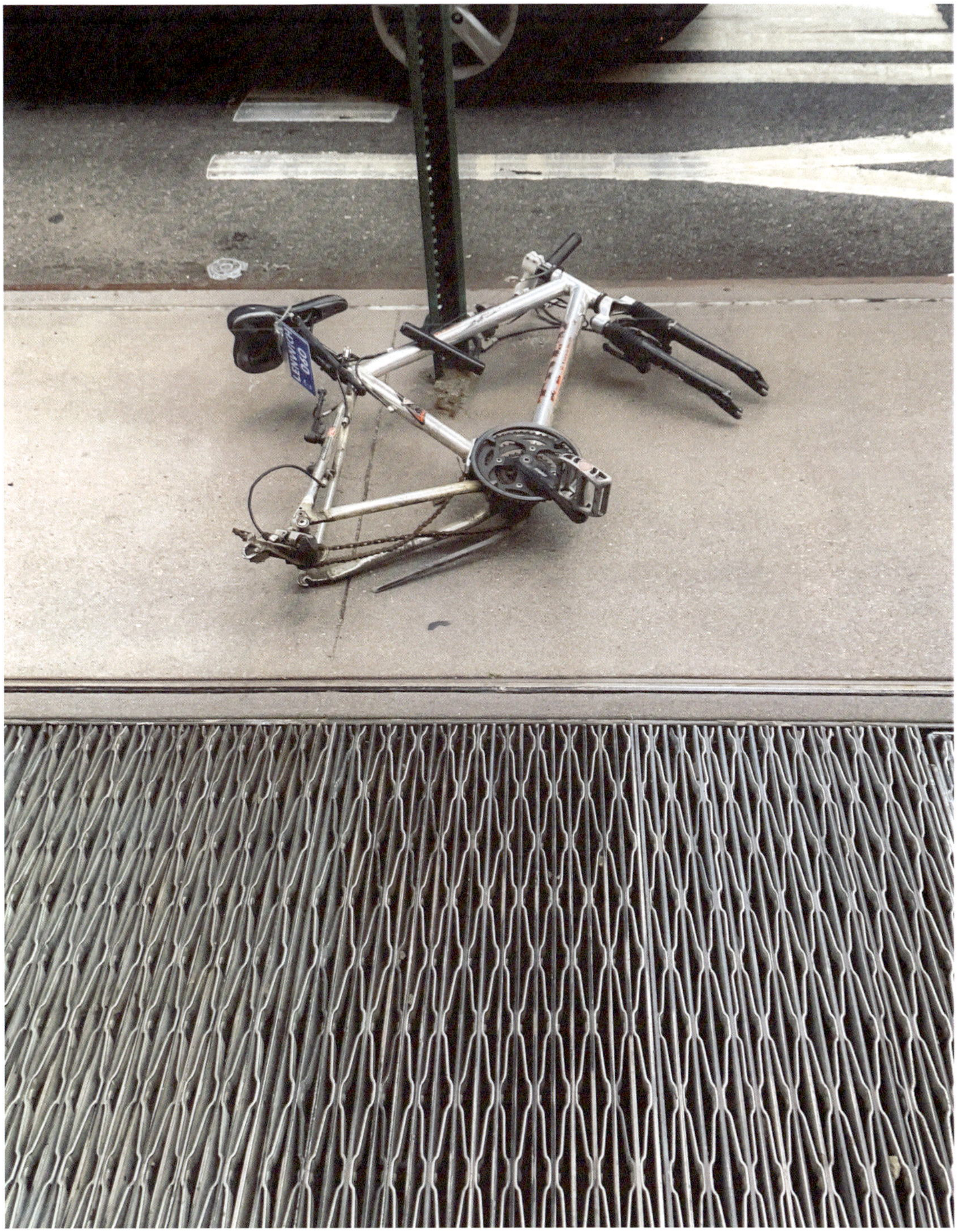

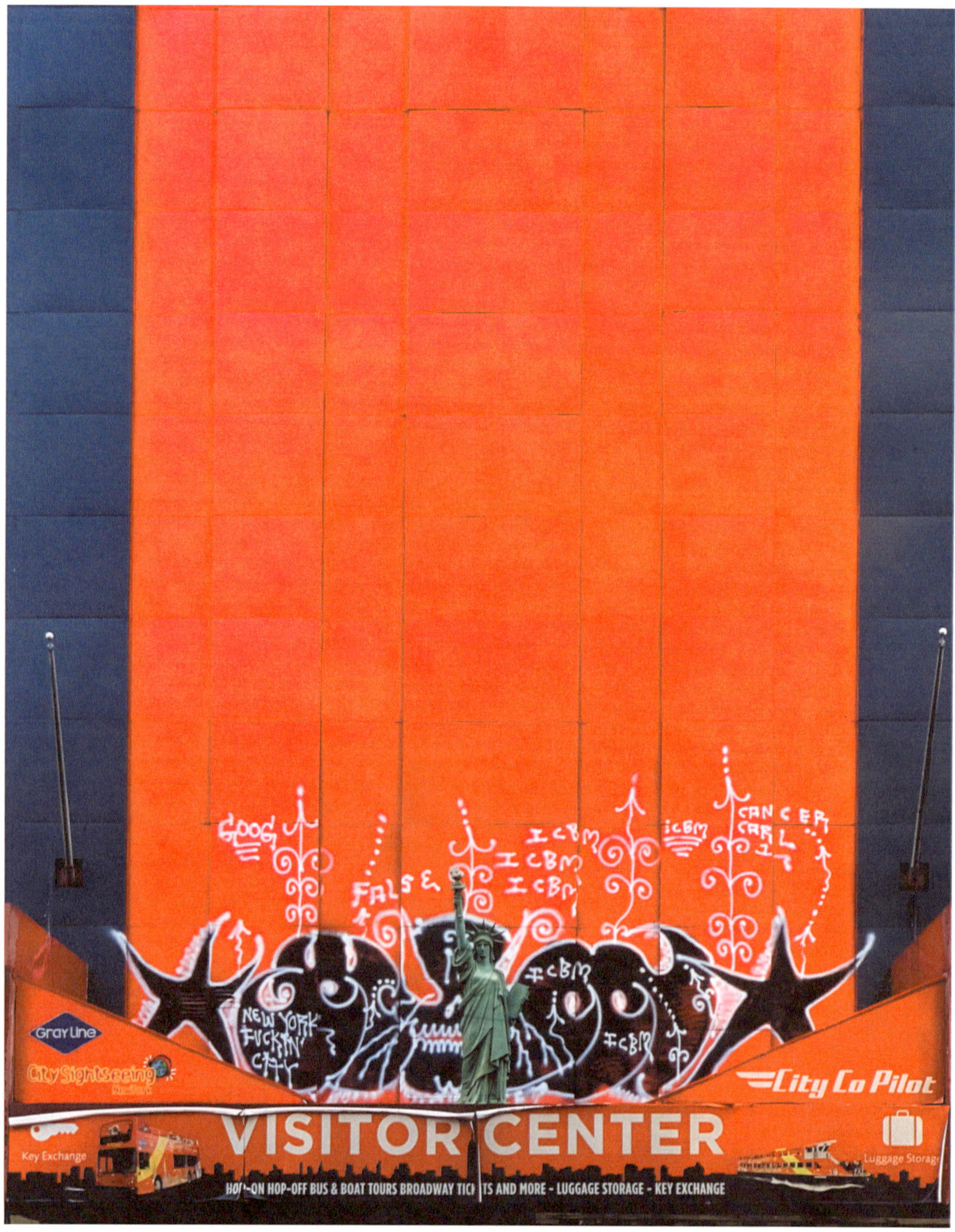

Gray Line
City Sightseeing New York
Key Exchange
City Co Pilot
Luggage Storage
VISITOR CENTER
HOP-ON HOP-OFF BUS & BOAT TOURS BROADWAY TICKETS AND MORE - LUGGAGE STORAGE - KEY EXCHANGE
NEW YORK FUCKIN' CITY
FALSE
ICBM
ICBM
ICBM
ICBM
ICBM
CANCER CARL
SOOS

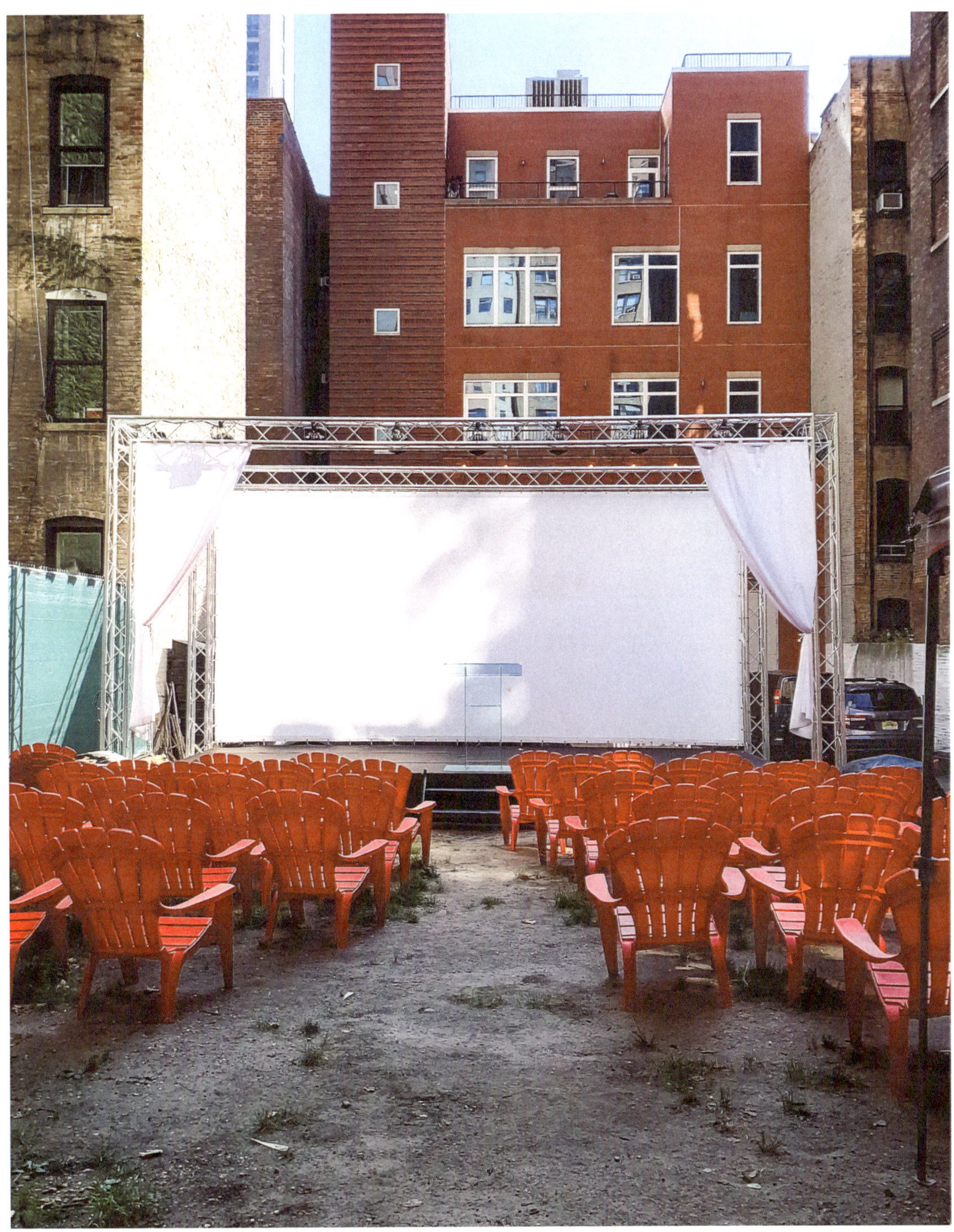

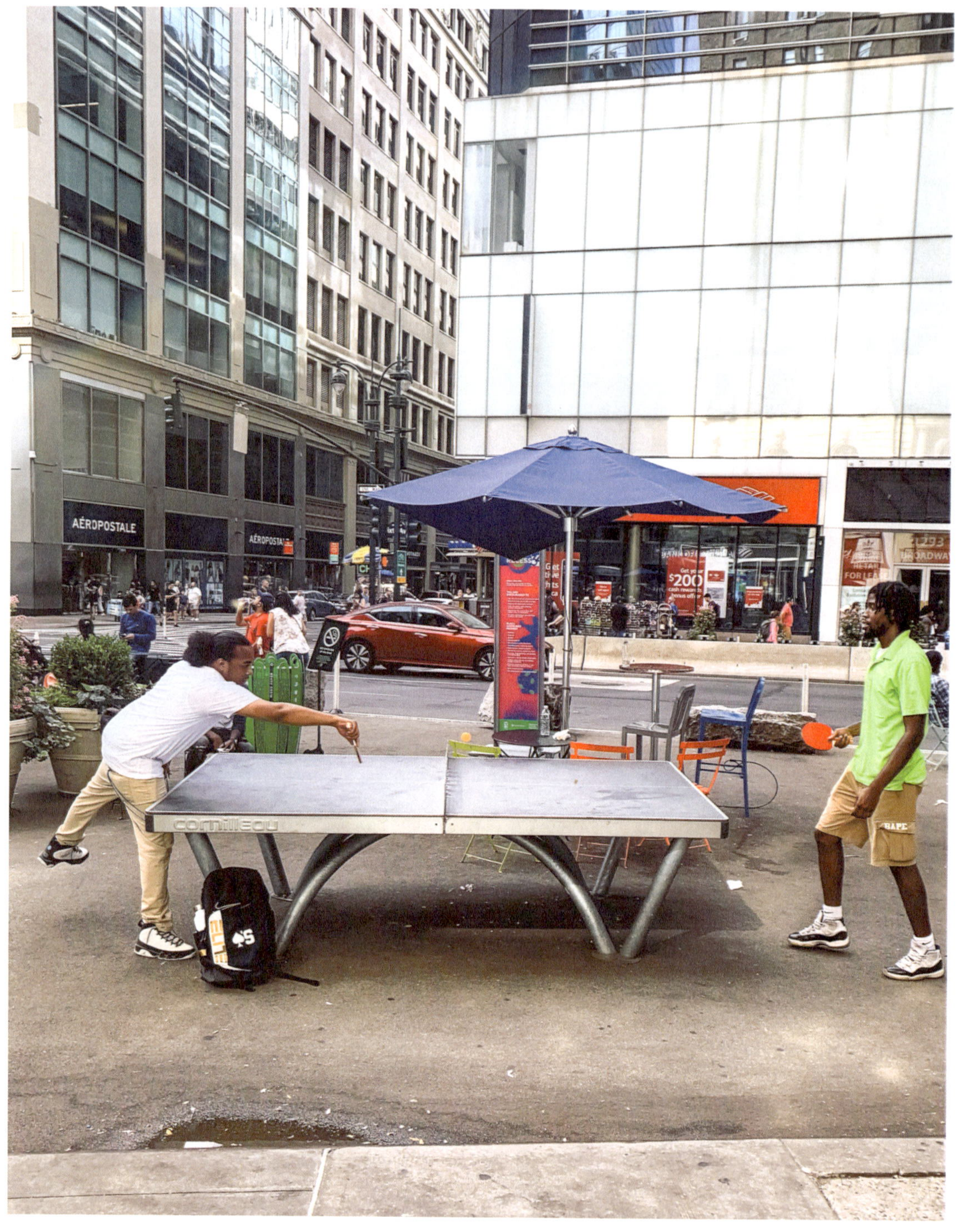

AÉROPOSTALE
AÉROPOSTALE
cornilleau

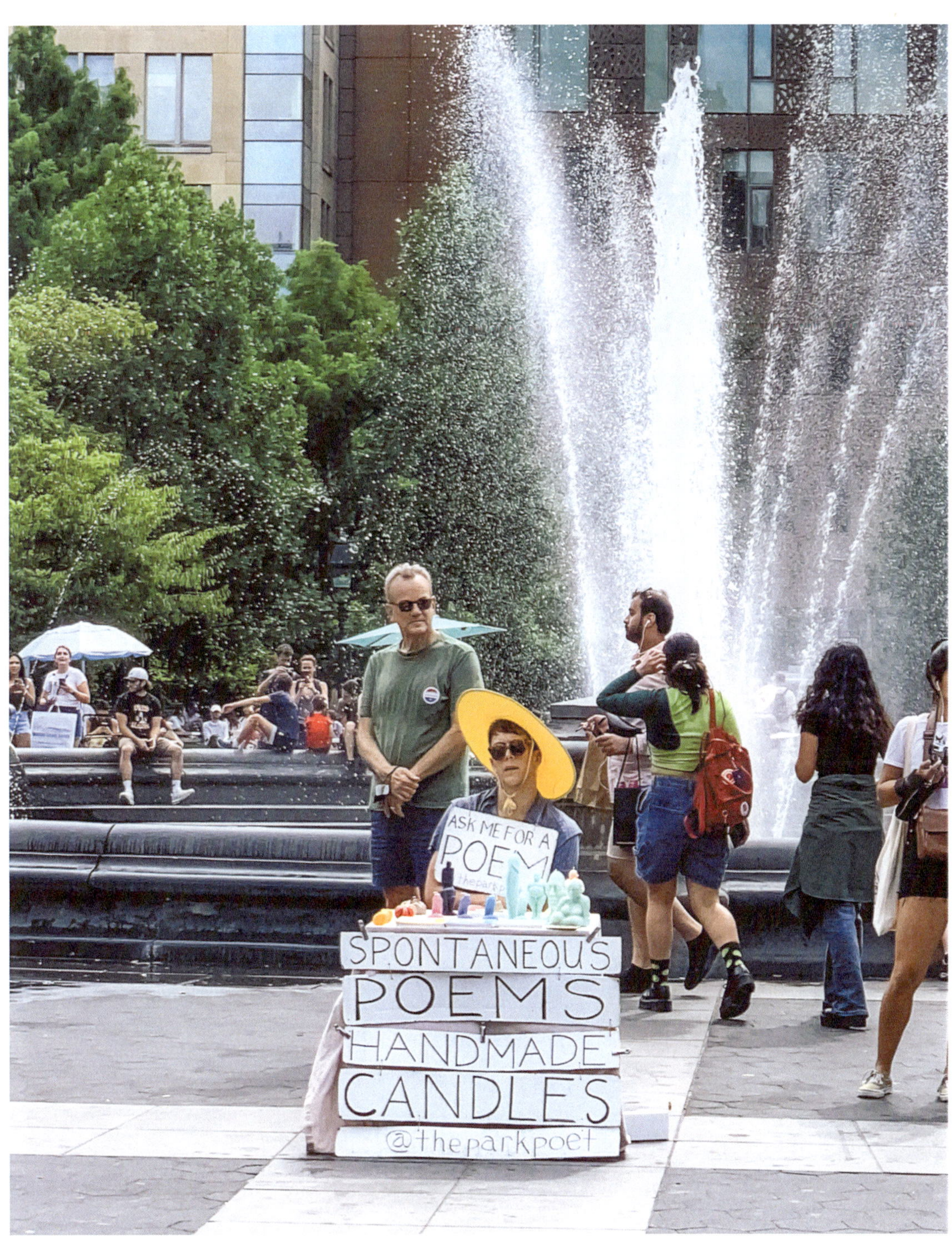

ASK ME FOR A
POEM
@thepark...
SPONTANEOUS
POEMS
HANDMADE
CANDLES
@theparkpoet

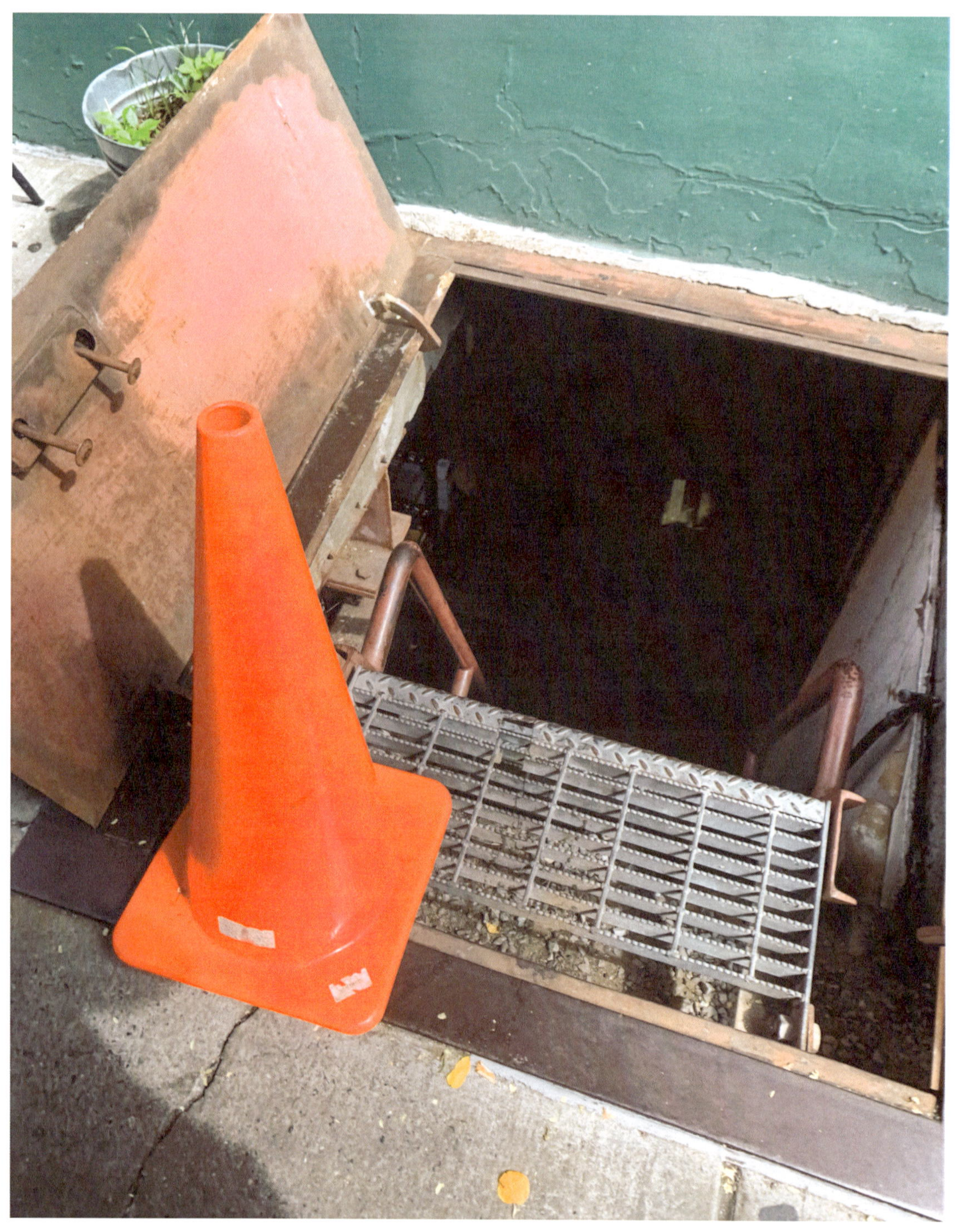

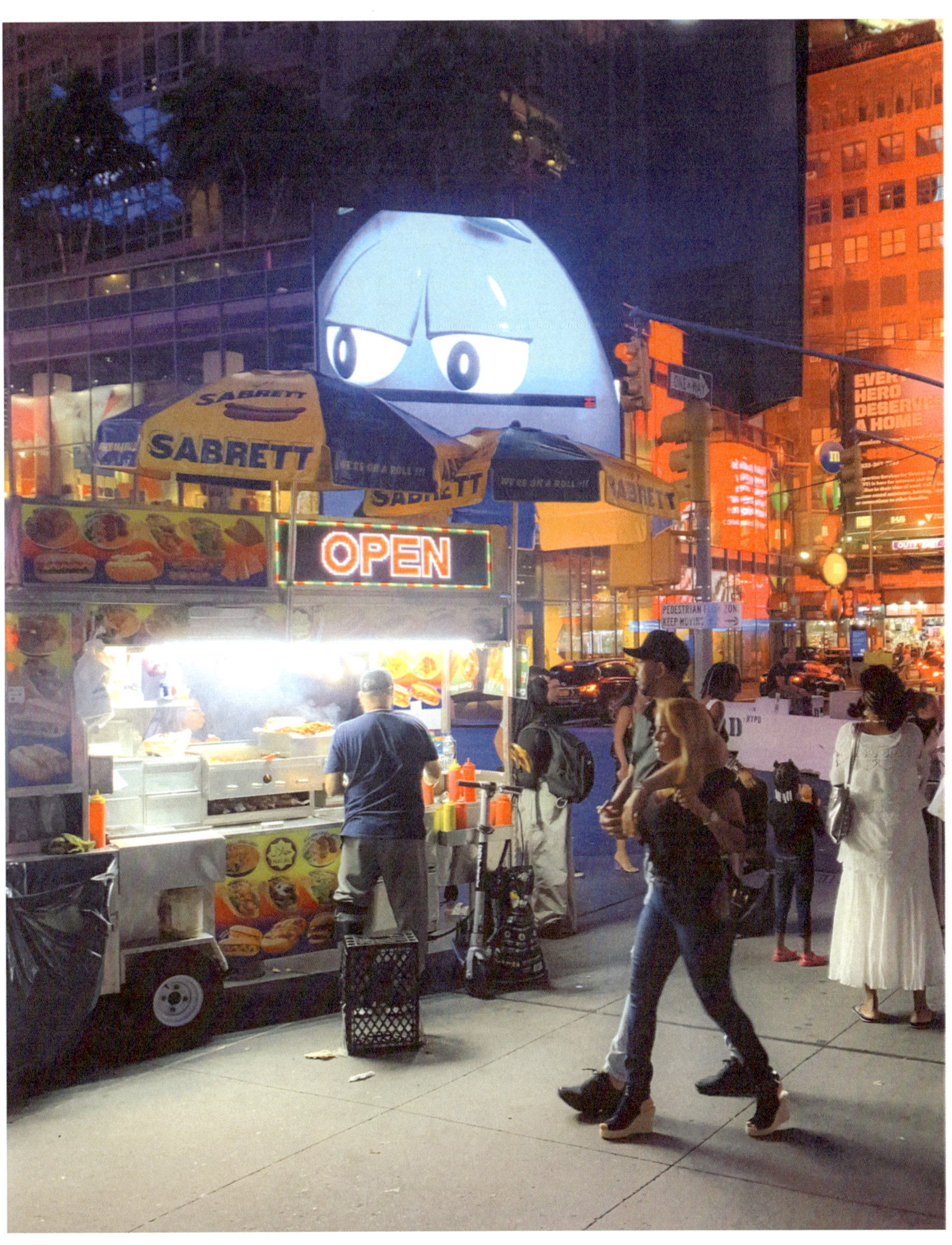

SABRETT
SABRETT
WE'RE ON A ROLL!!!
WE'RE ON A ROLL!!!
SABRETT
SABRETT
OPEN
EVERY
HERO
DESERVES
A HOME
PEDESTRIAN ZONE
KEEP MOVING
NYPD

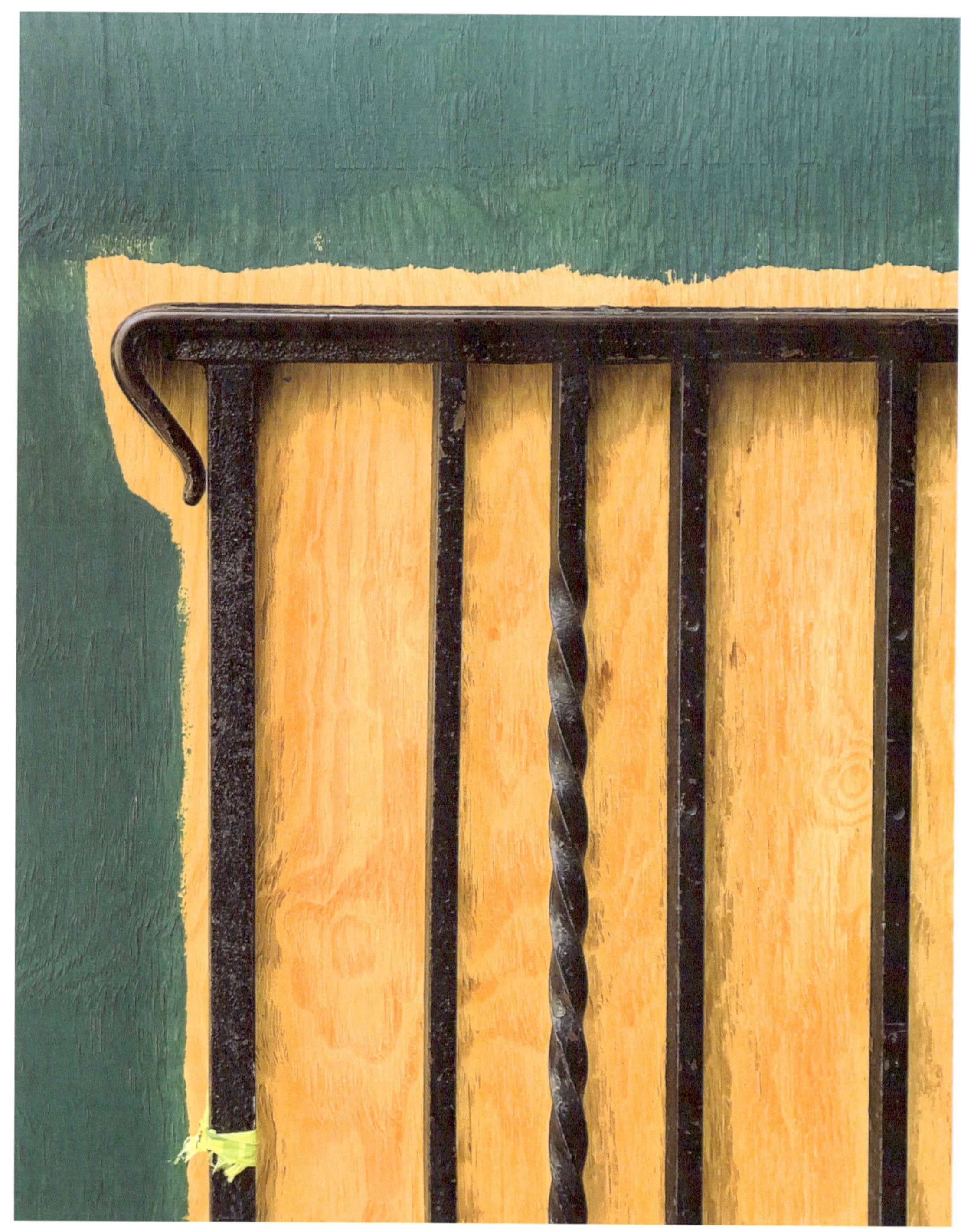

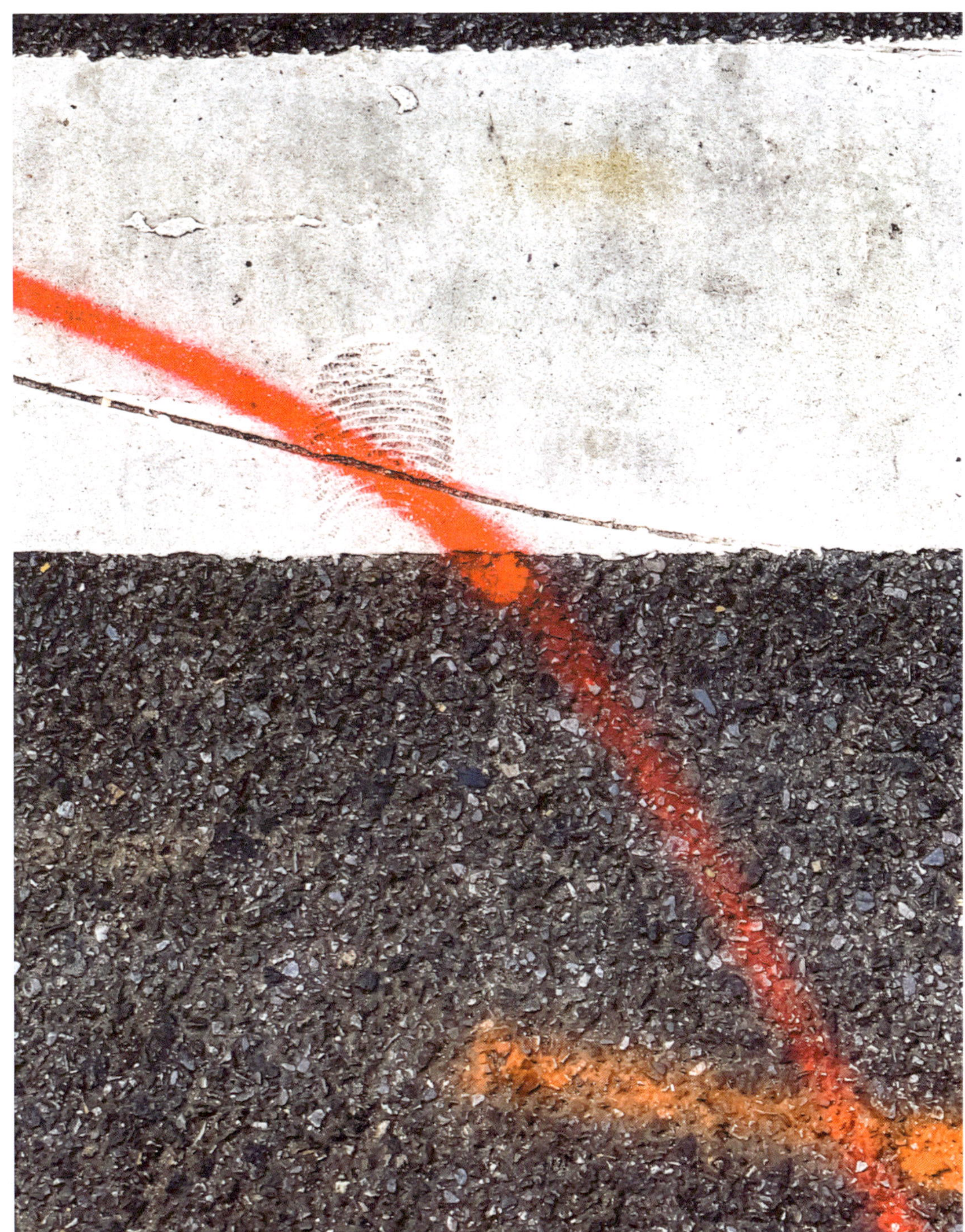

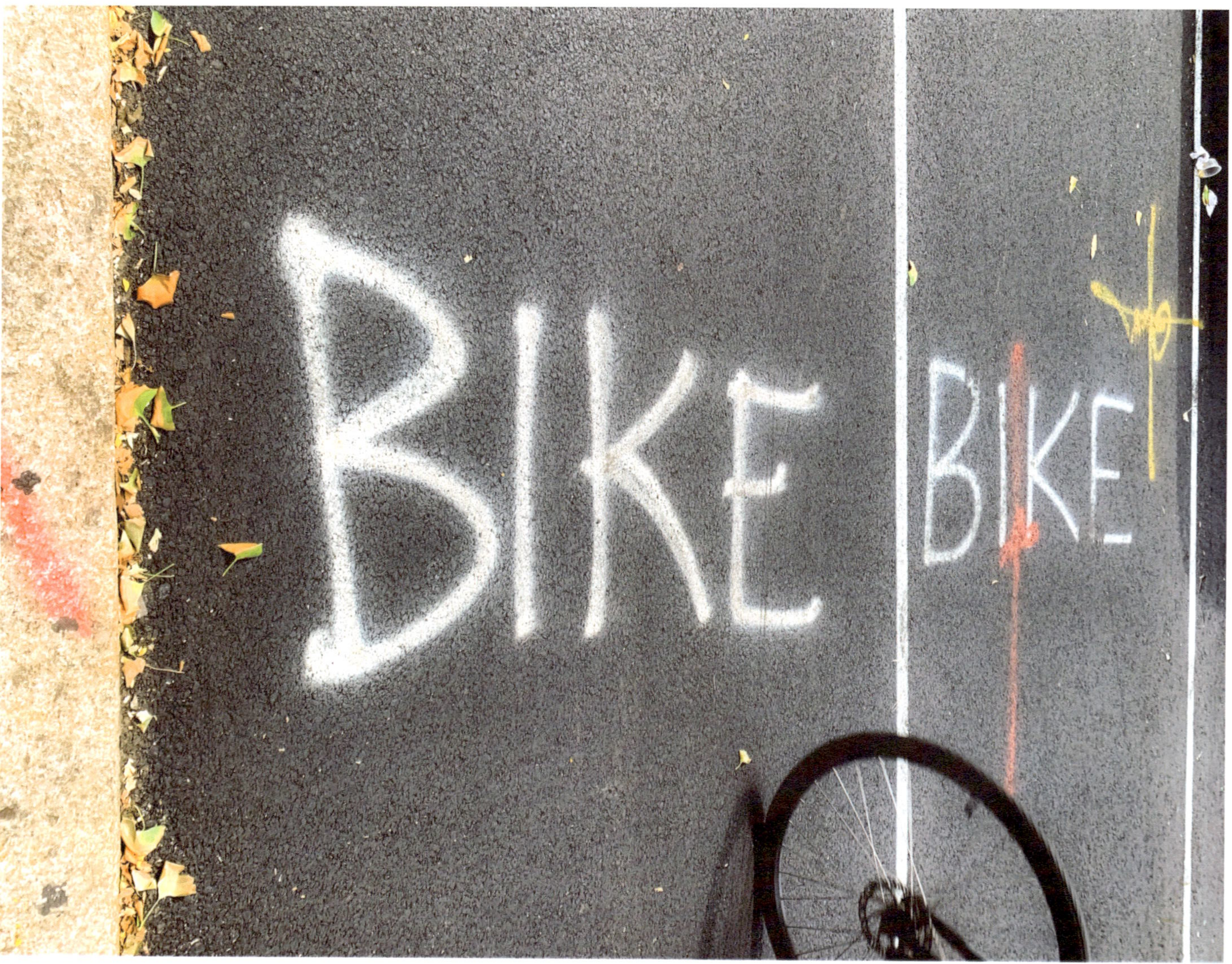

BIKE
BIKE

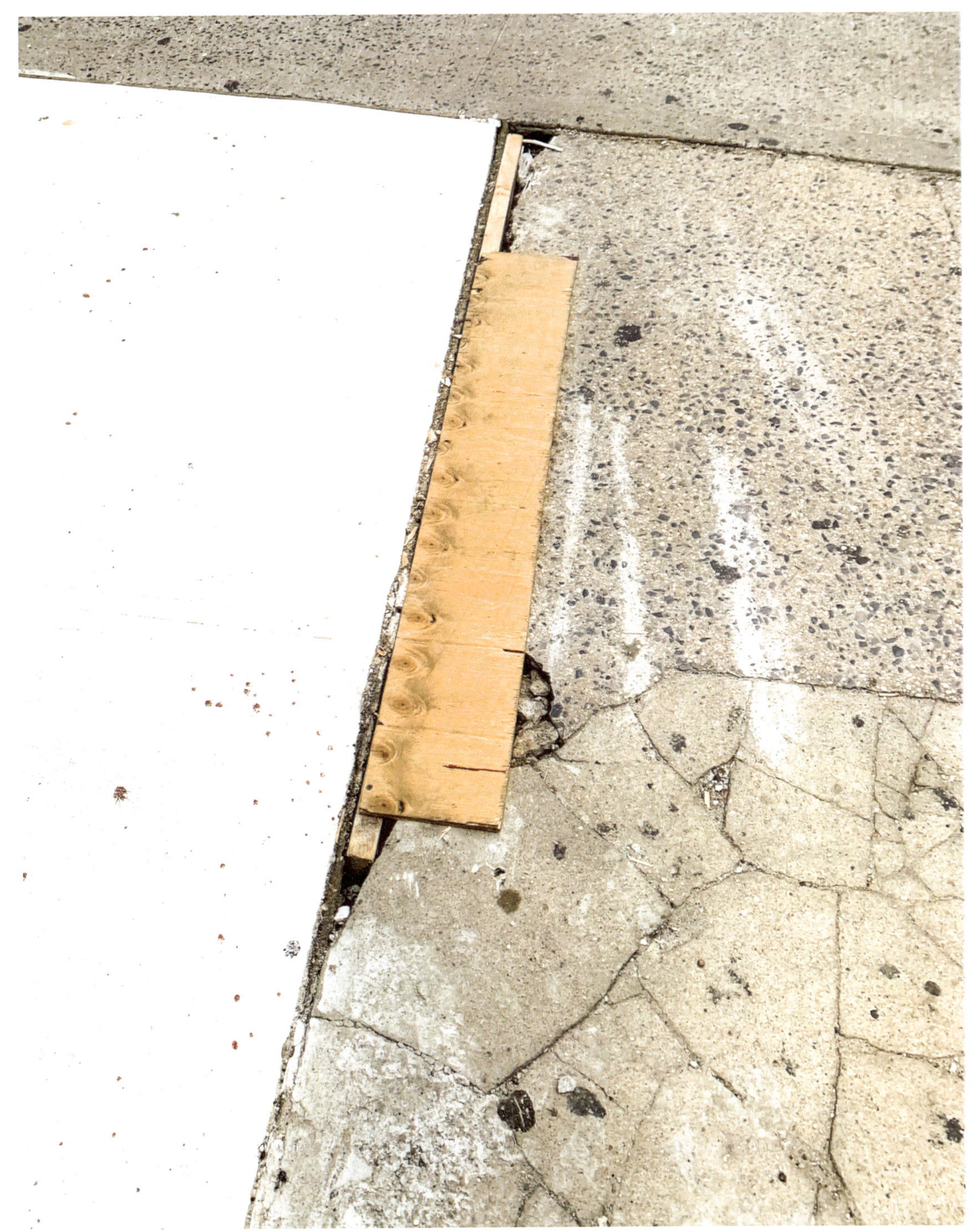

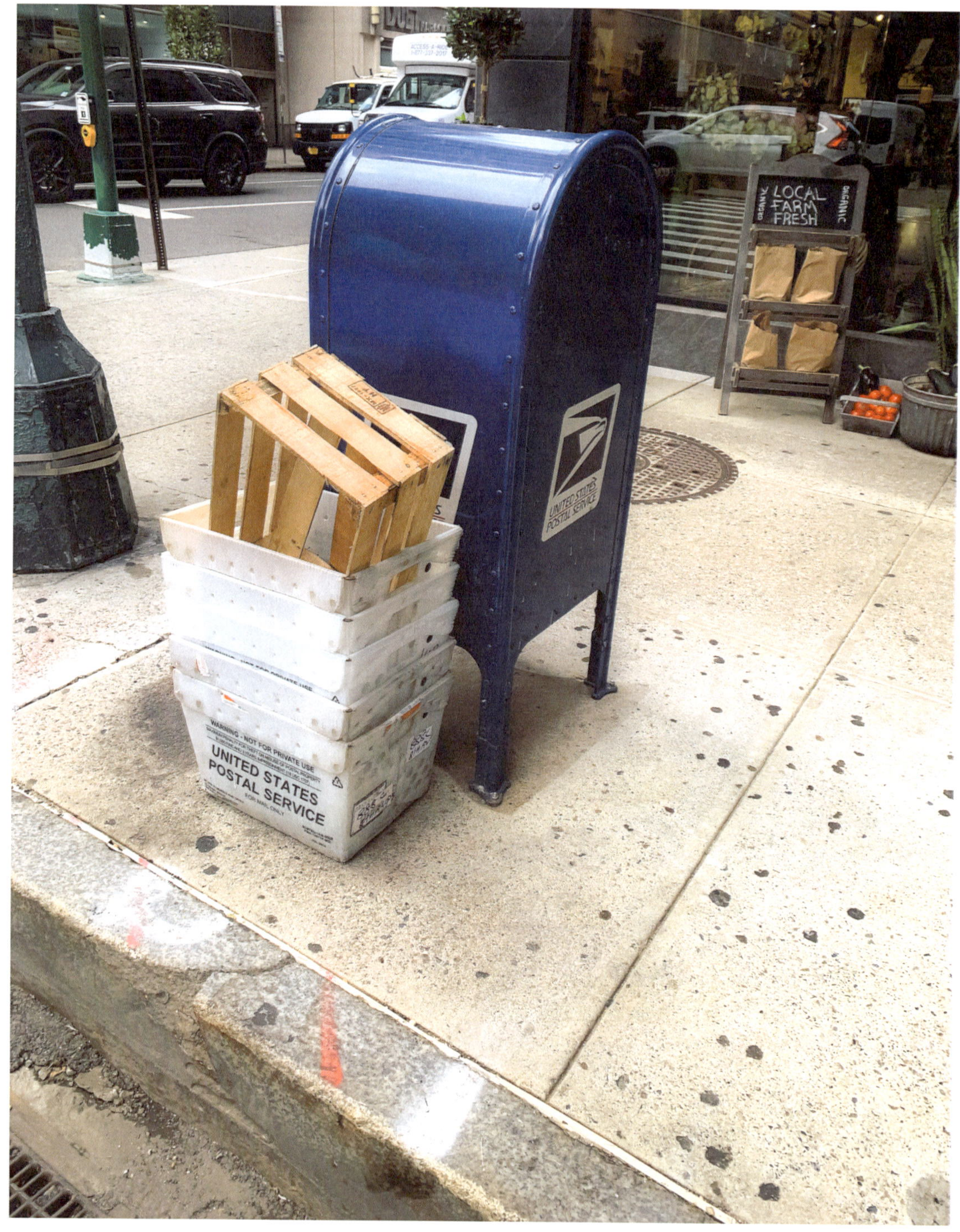
UNITED STATES
POSTAL SERVICE
WARNING - NOT FOR PRIVATE USE
UNITED STATES
POSTAL SERVICE
FOR MAIL ONLY
LOCAL
FARM
FRESH
ORGANIC
ORGANIC

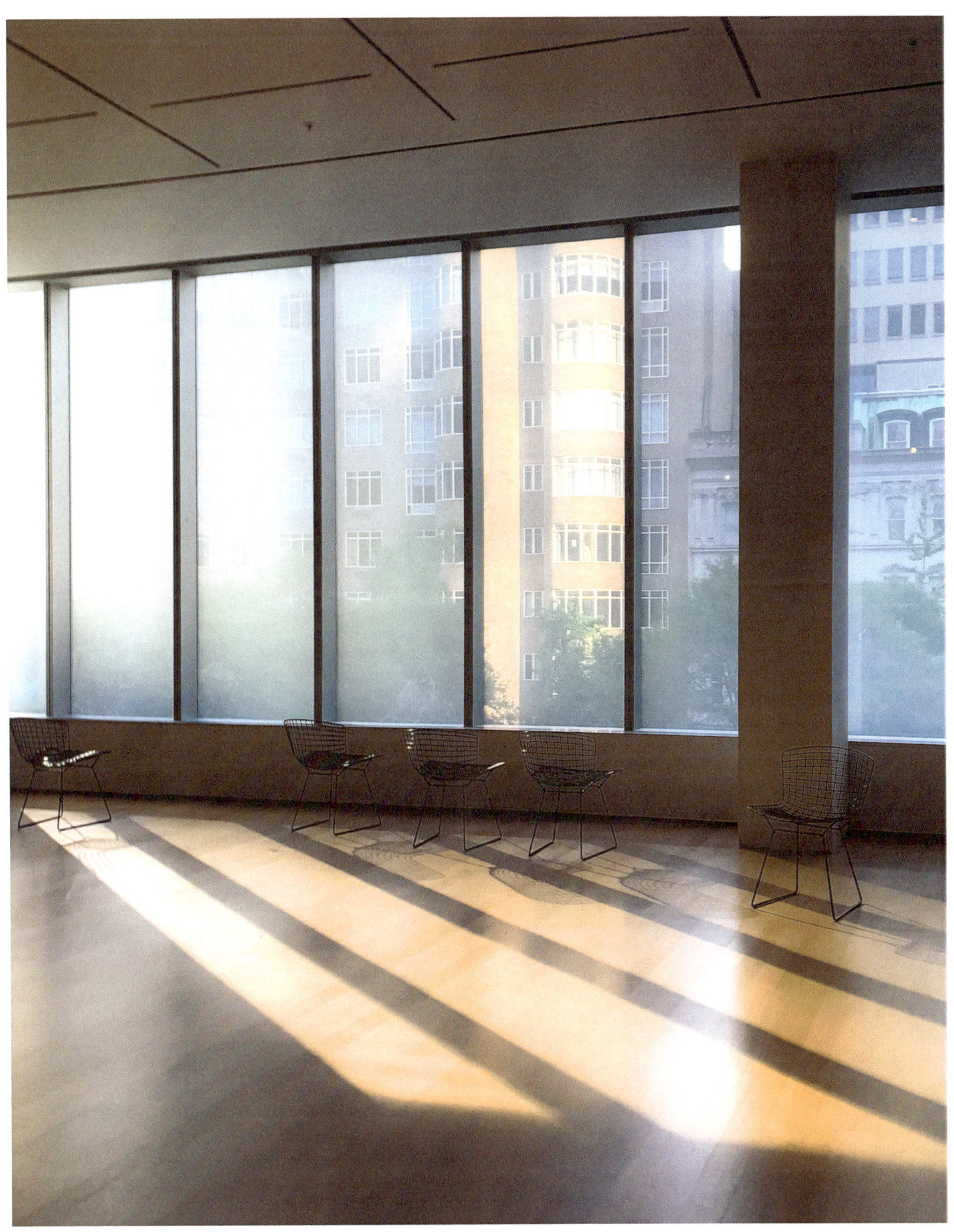

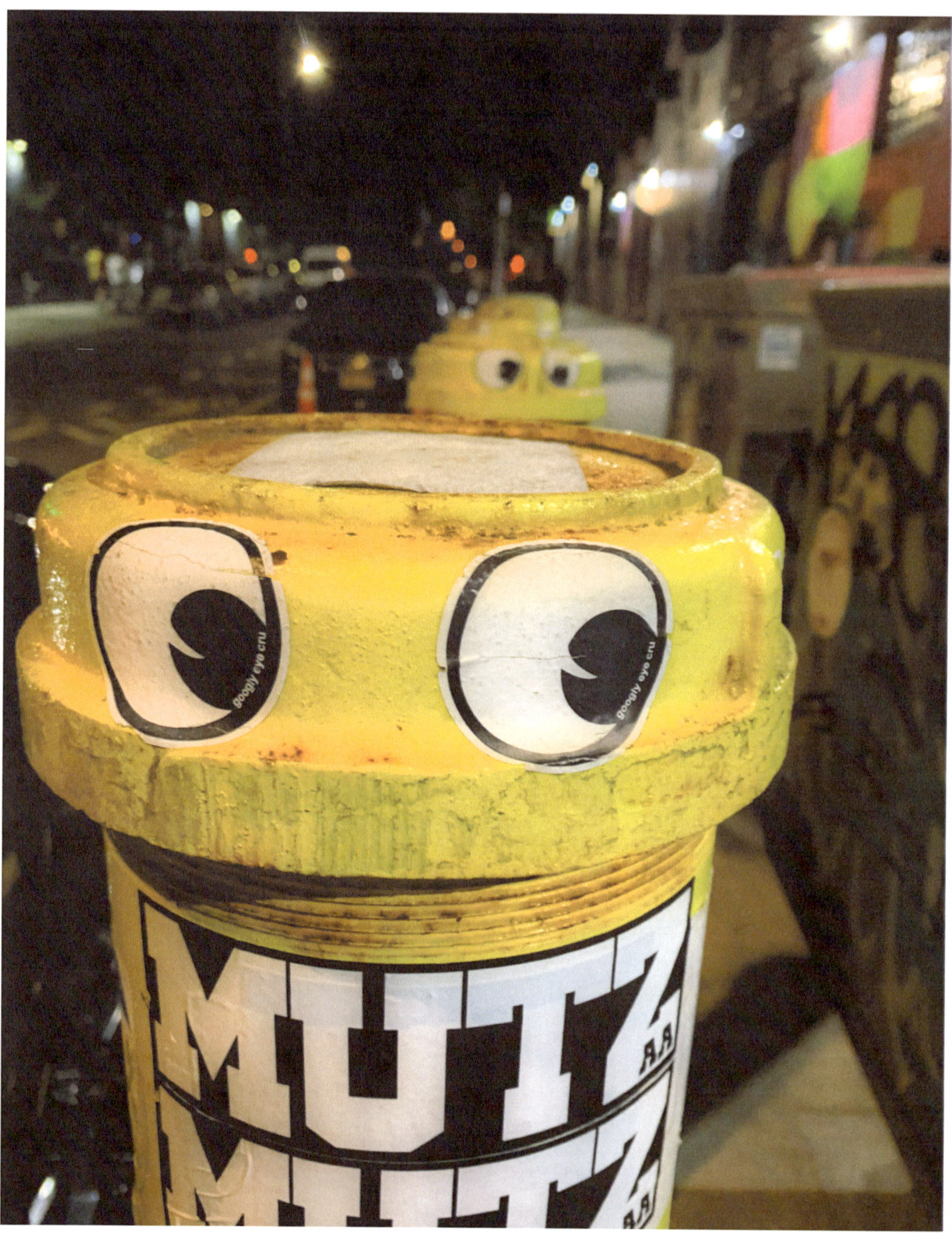

googly eye cru
googly eye cru
MUTZ
MUTZ

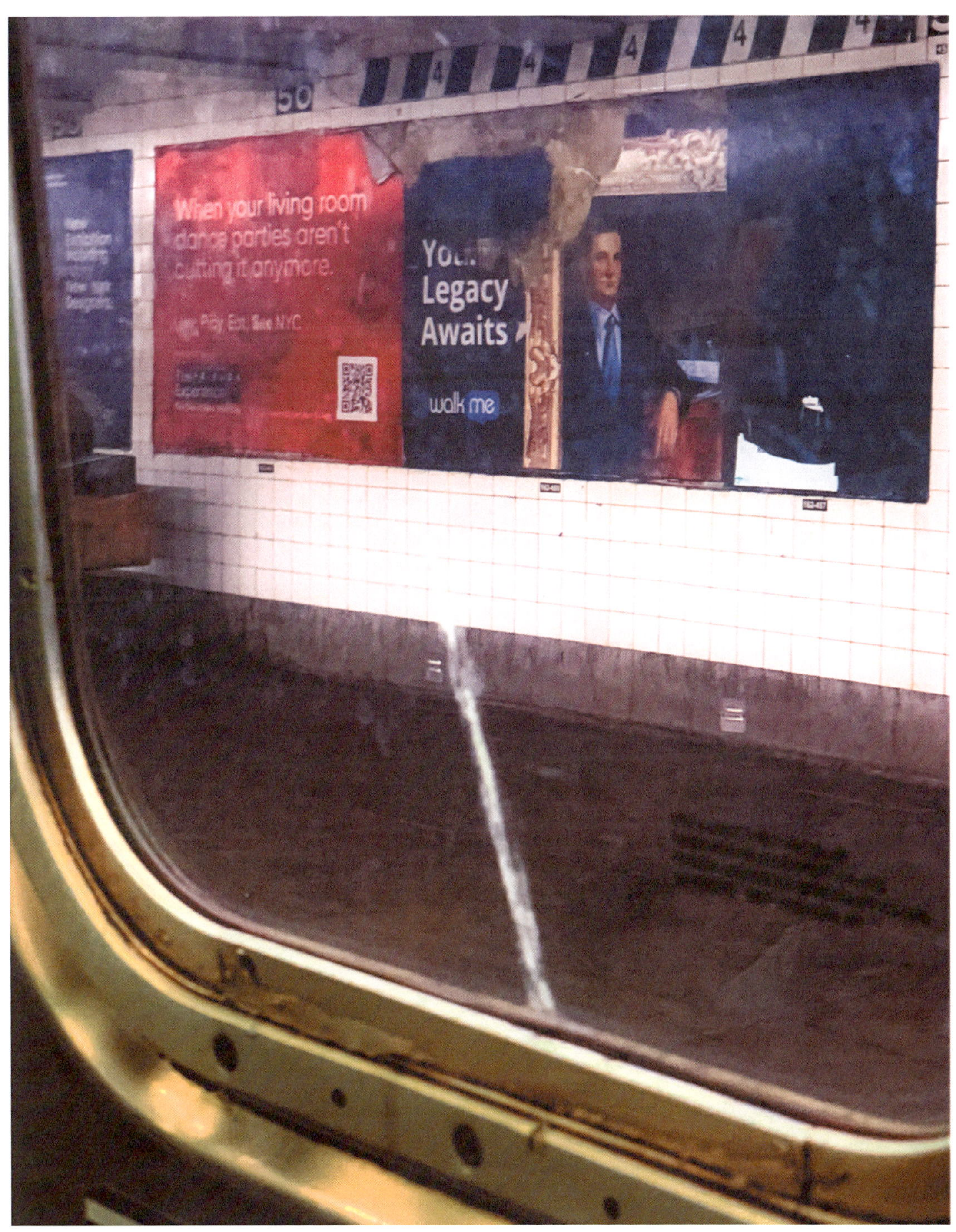
50
When your living room
dance parties aren't
cutting it anymore.
Play Eat. See NYC.
You.
Legacy
Awaits
walk me

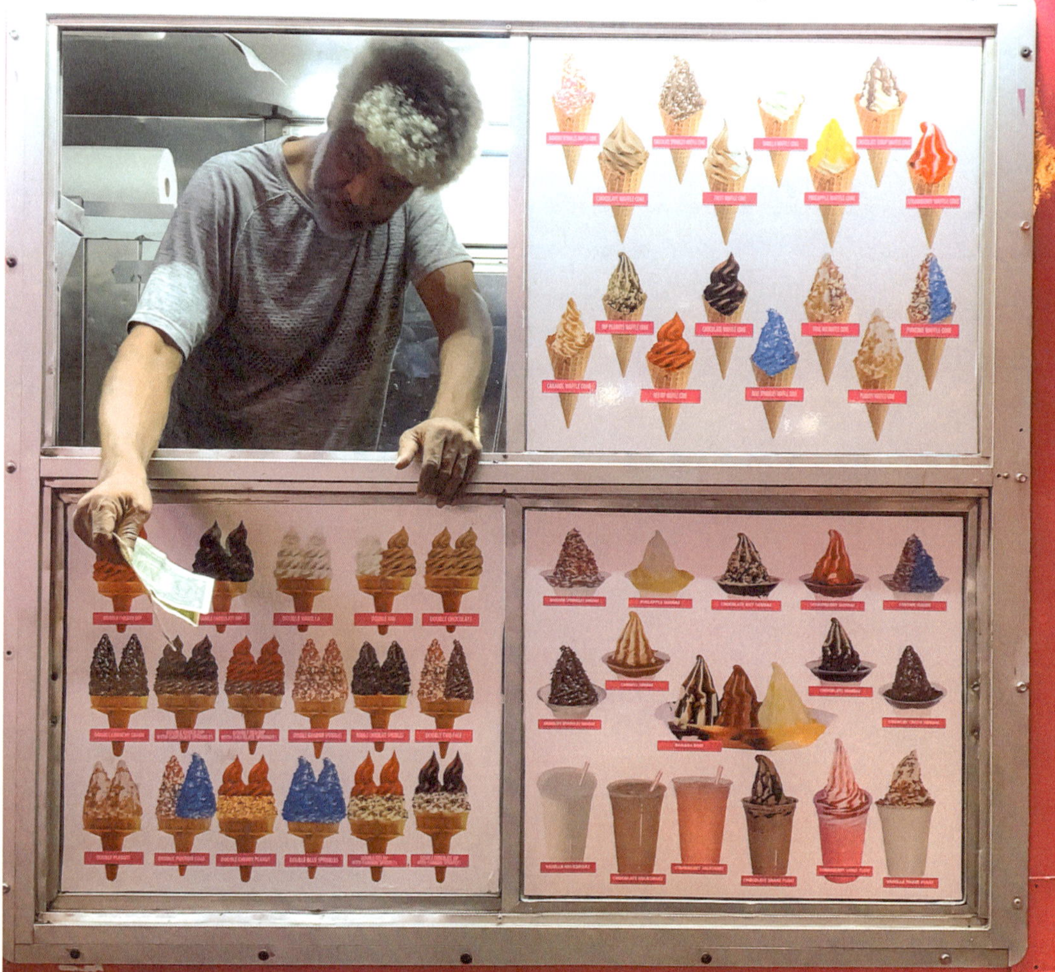
ES SHAKES CONES

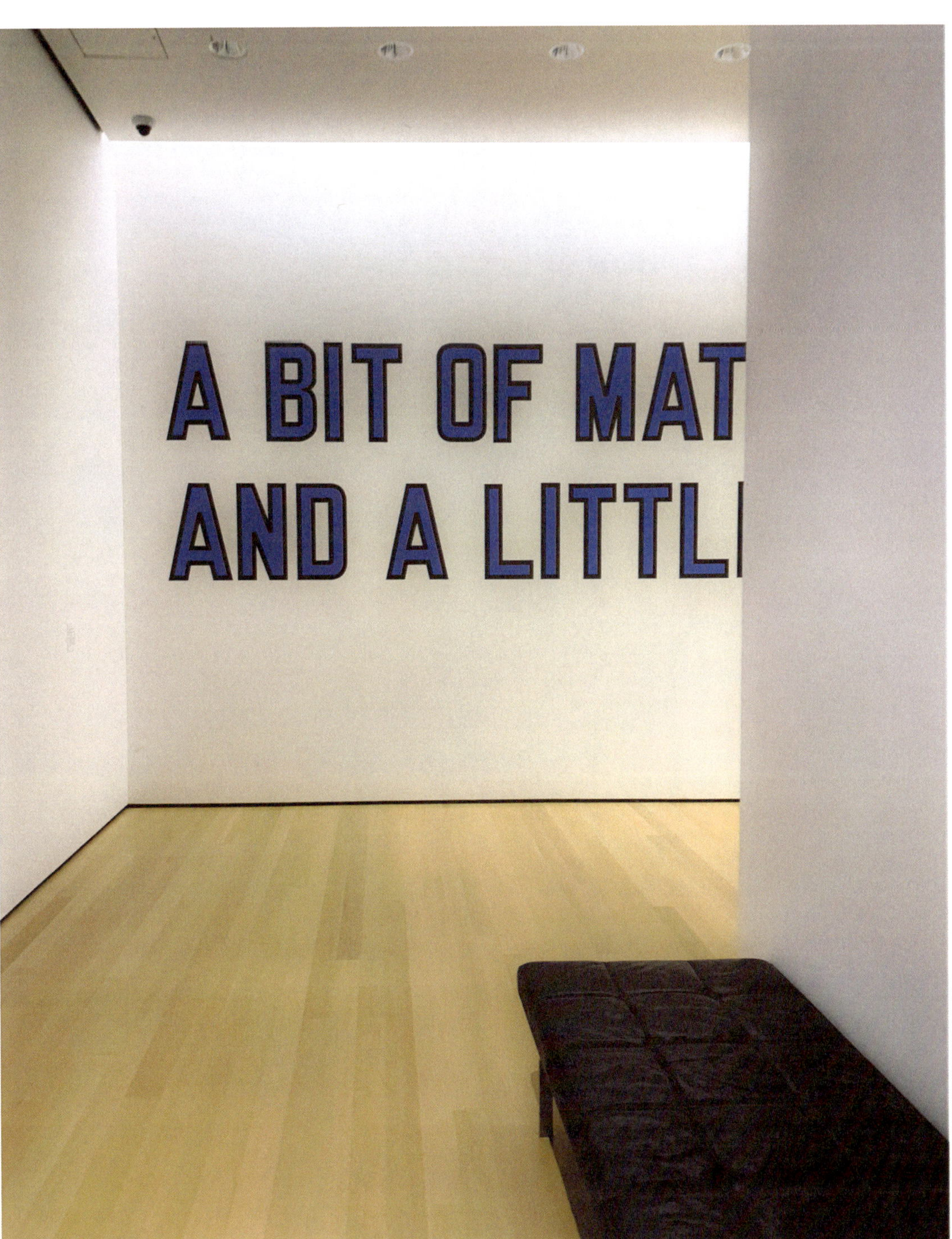

A BIT OF MAT
AND A LITTL

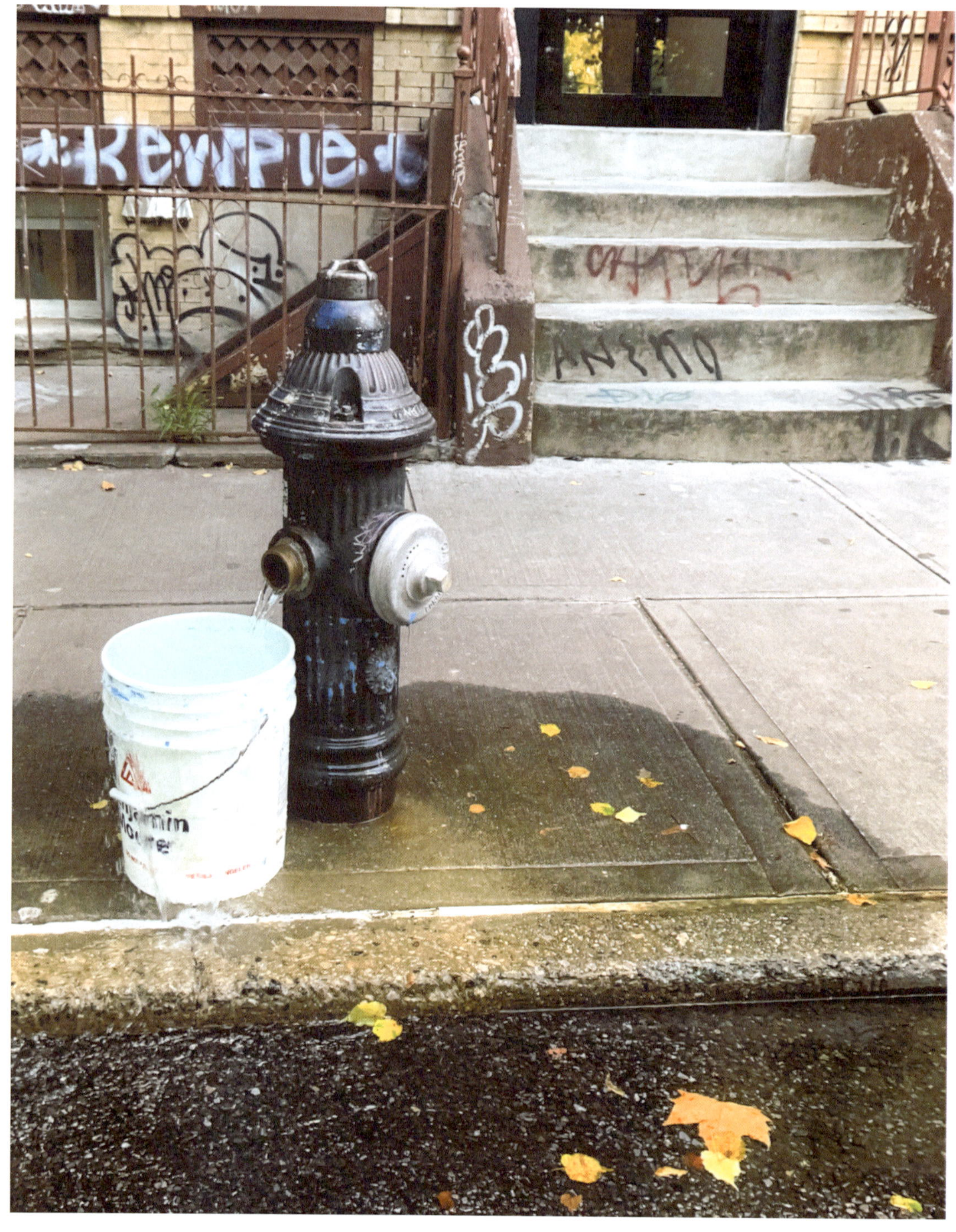

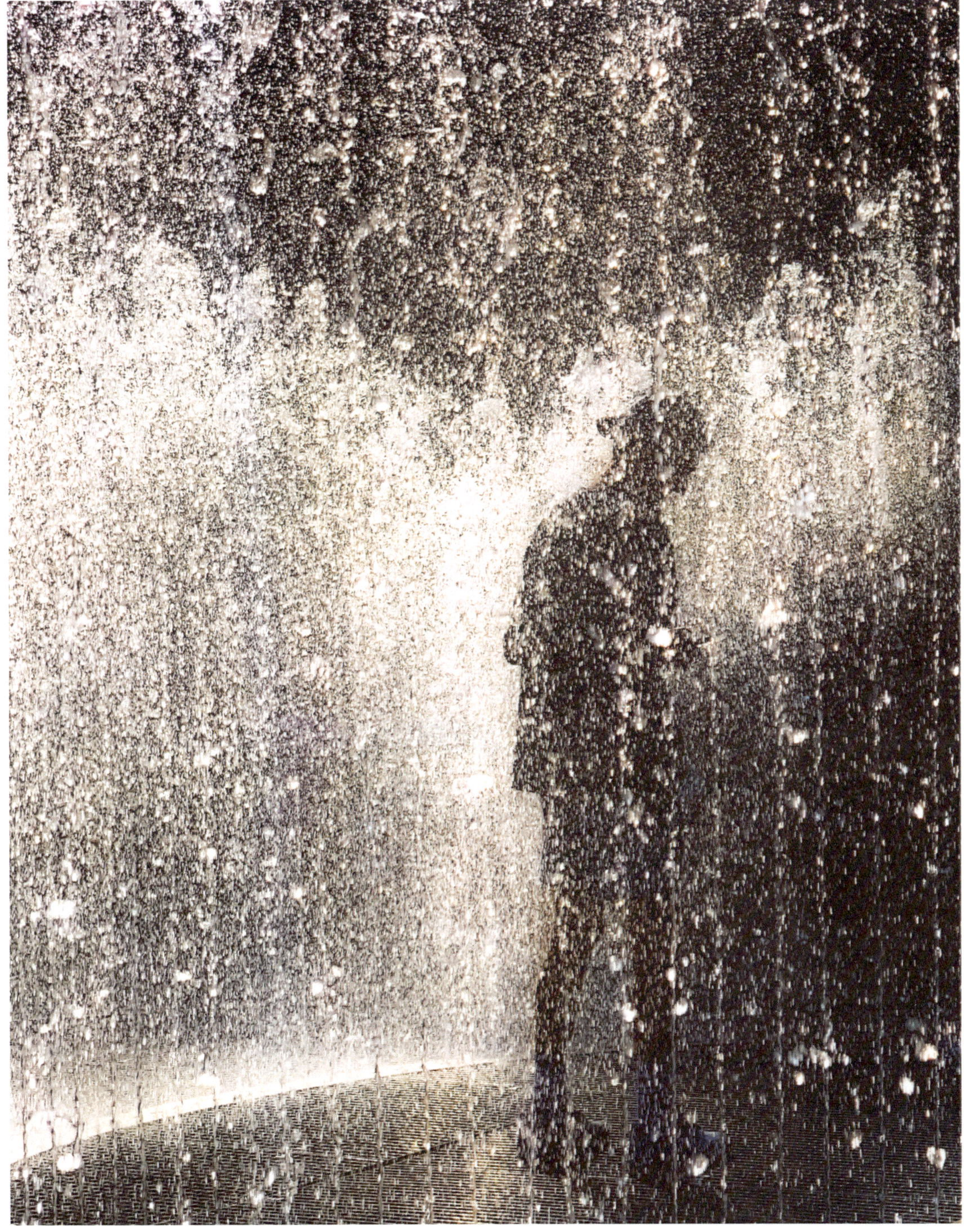

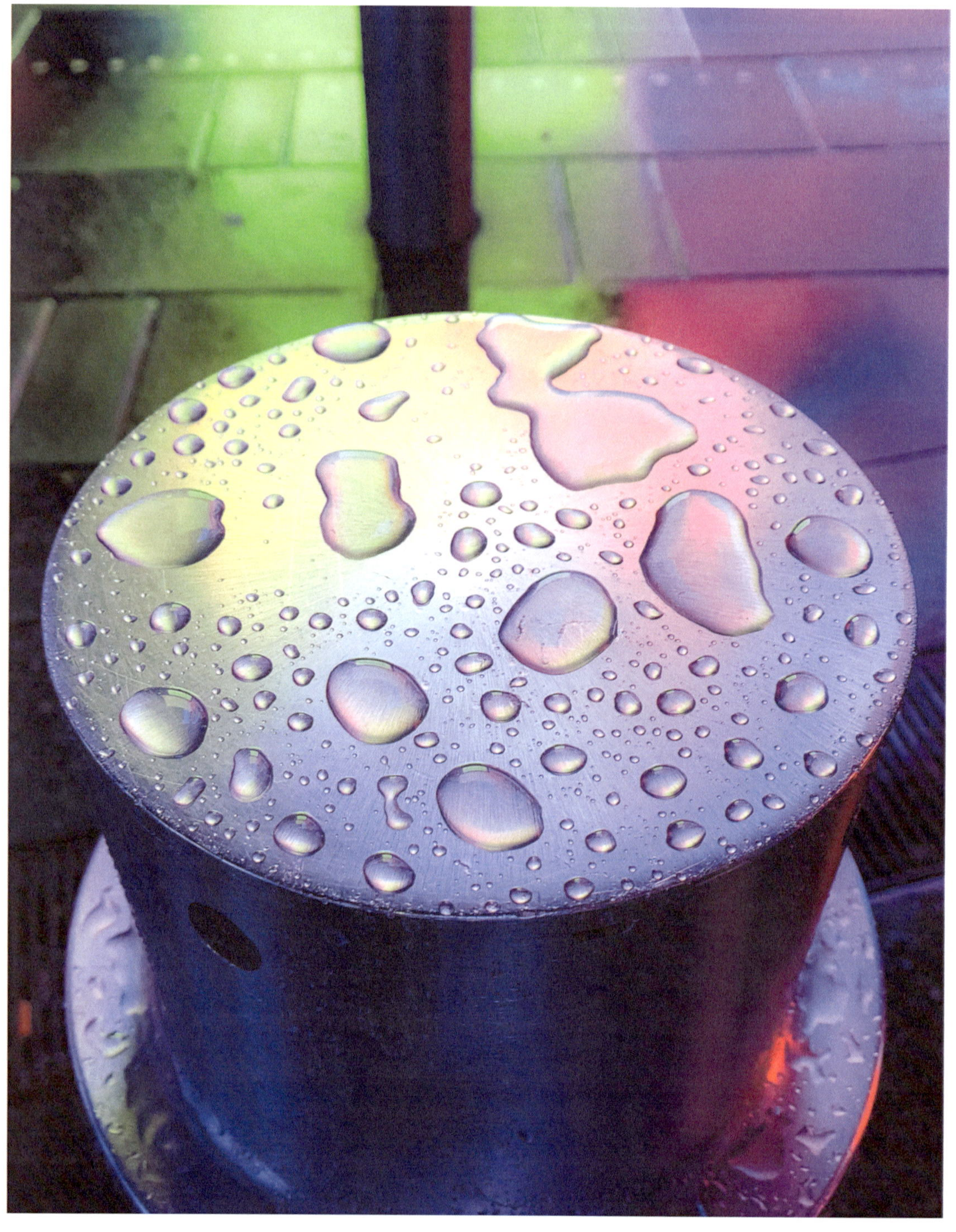

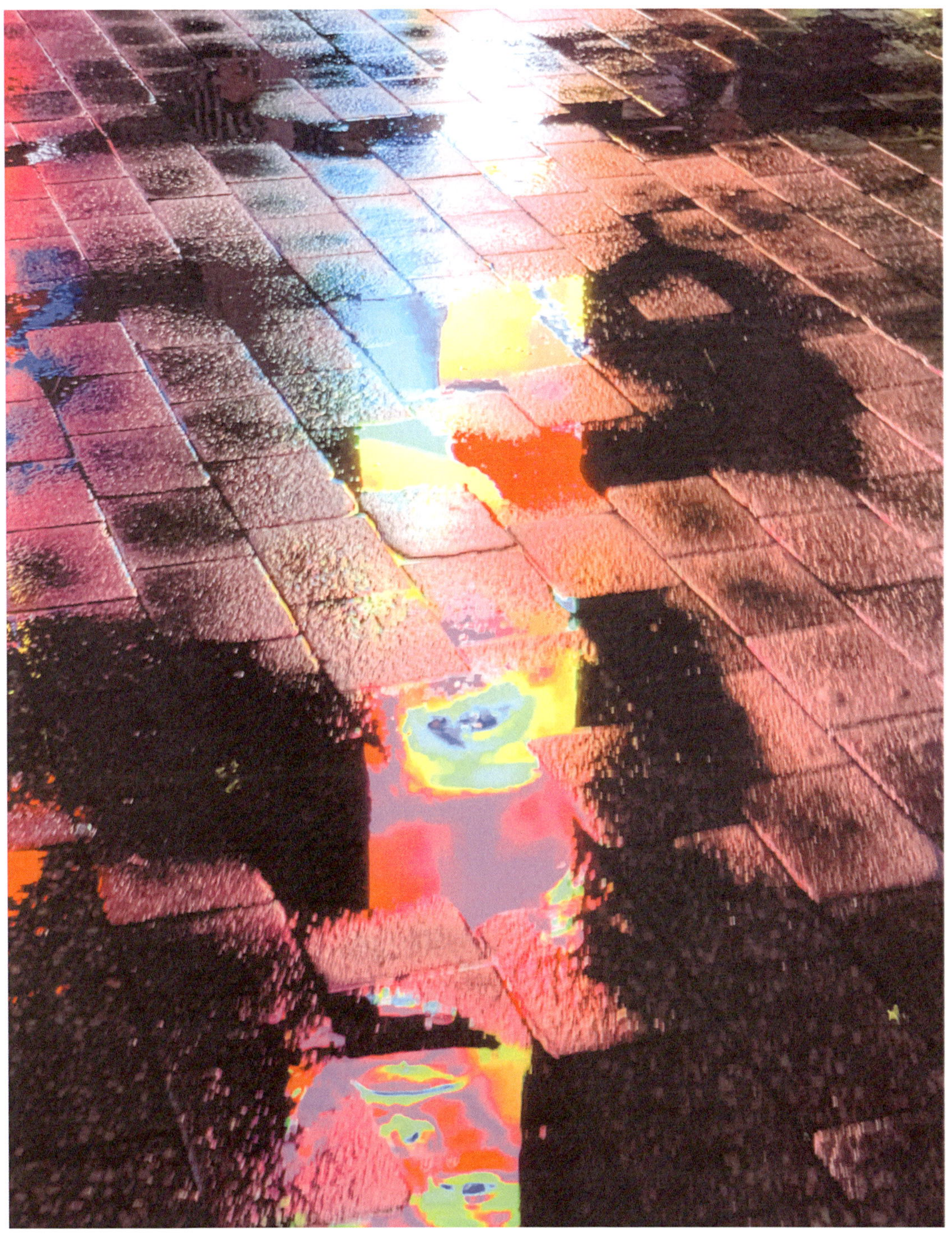

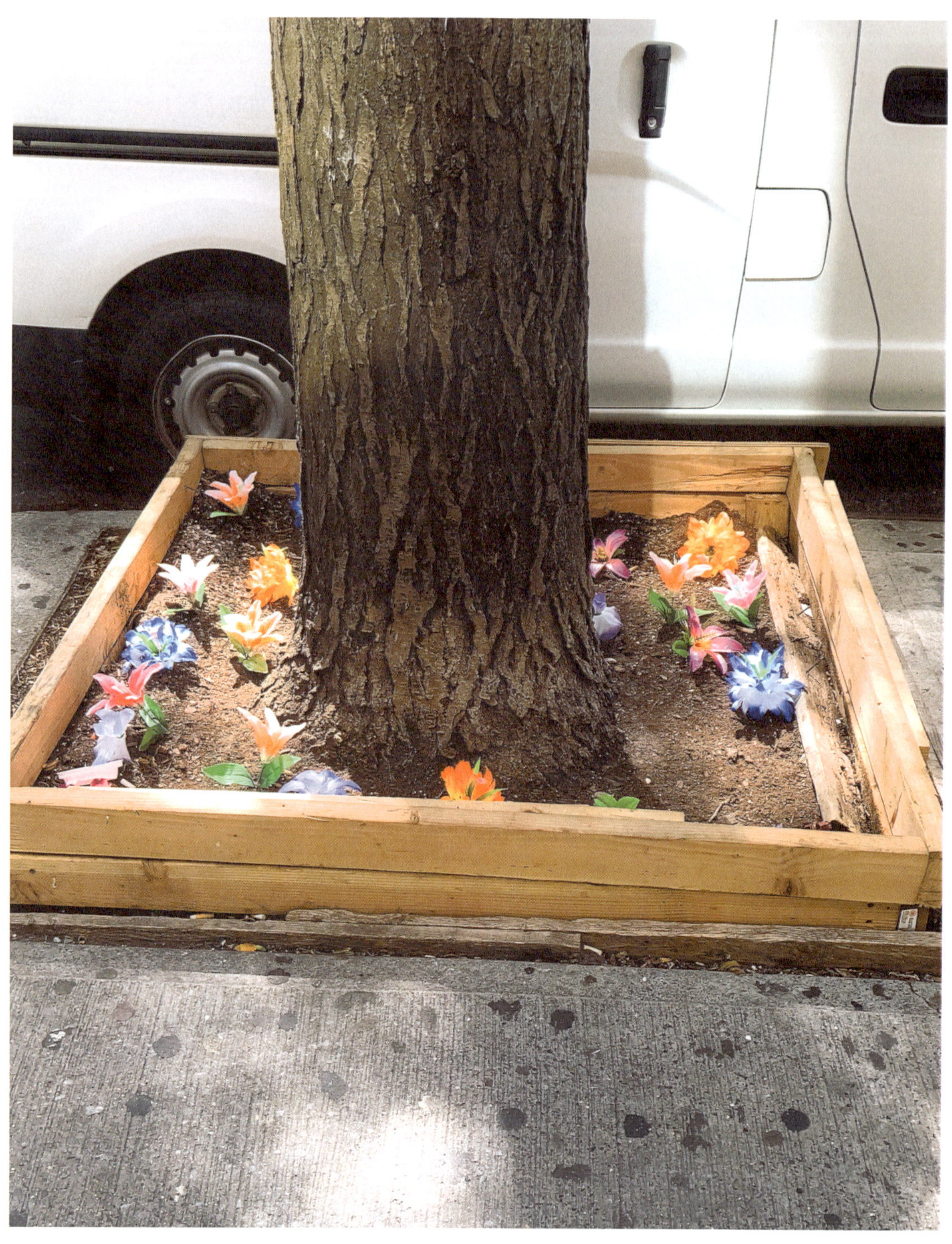

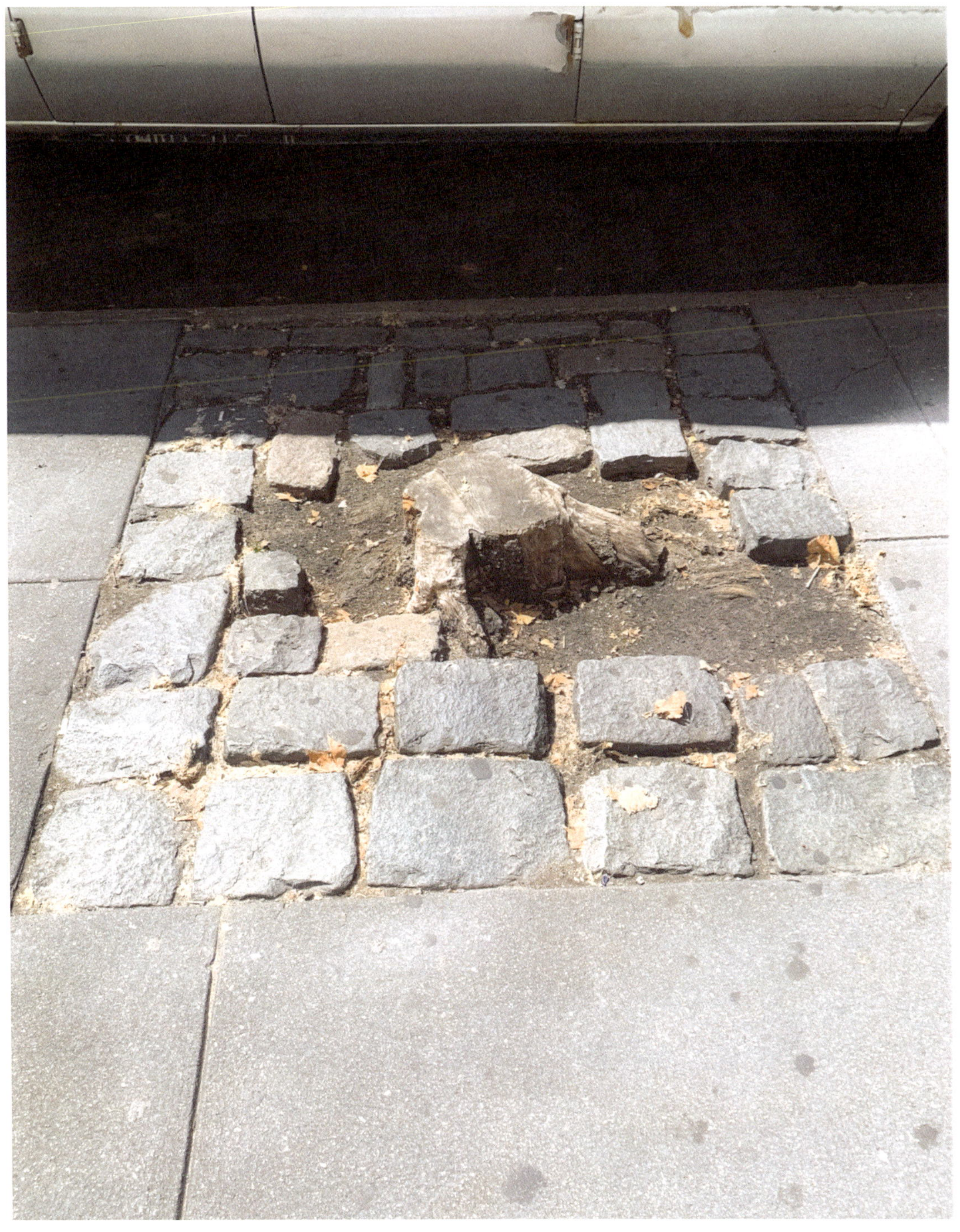

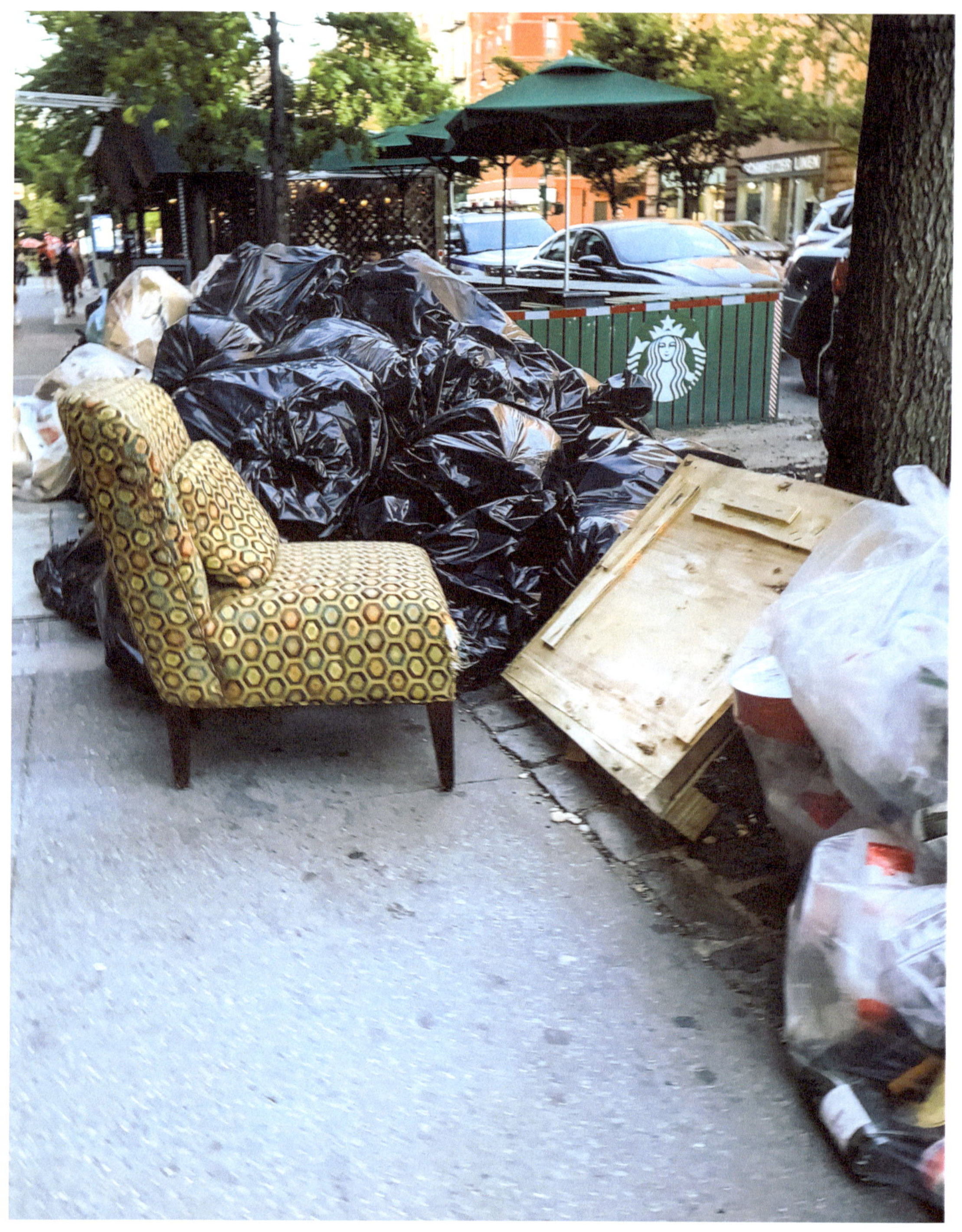

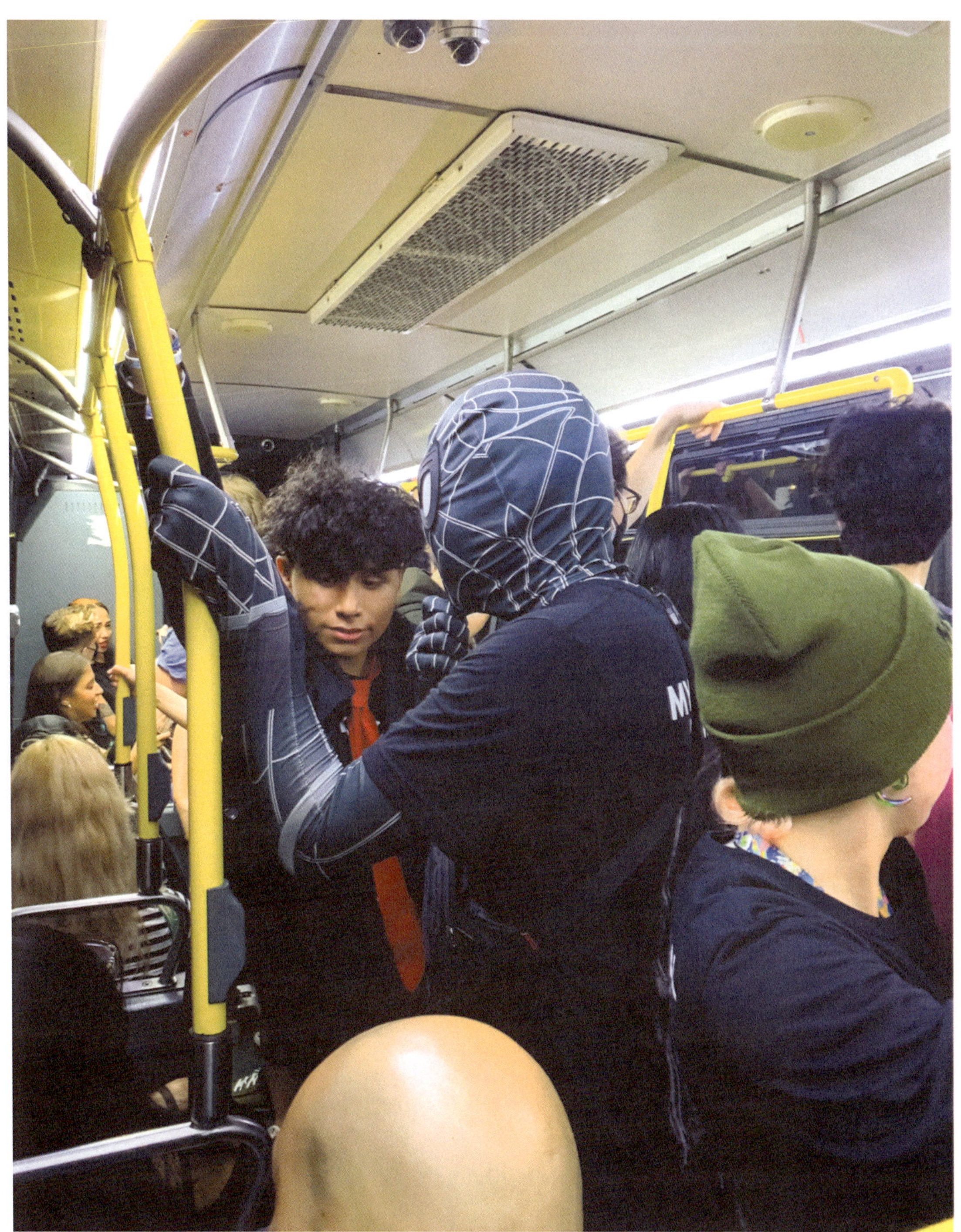

AROINT THEE
FOUL DEMON
HEK
TAD

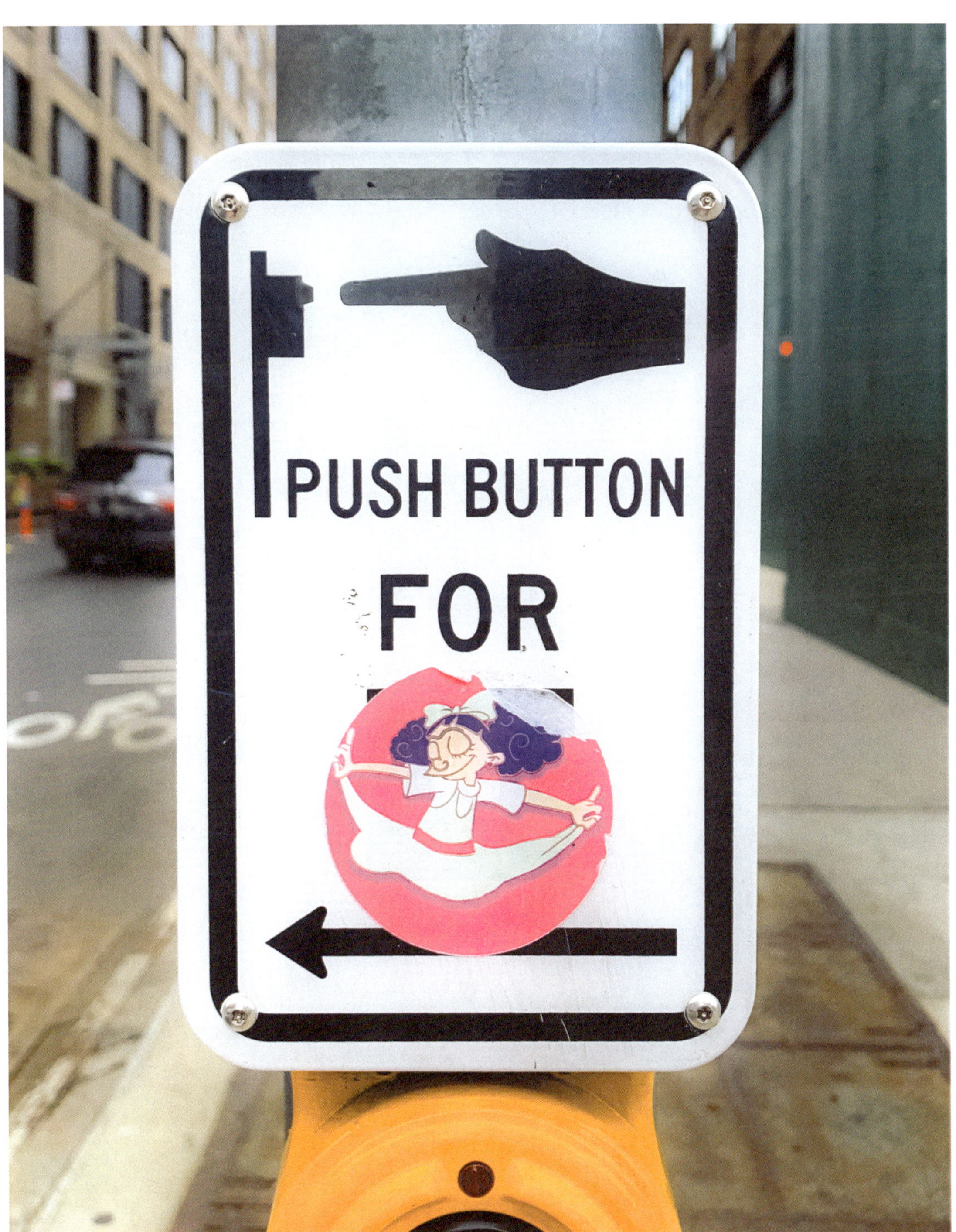
PUSH BUTTON
FOR

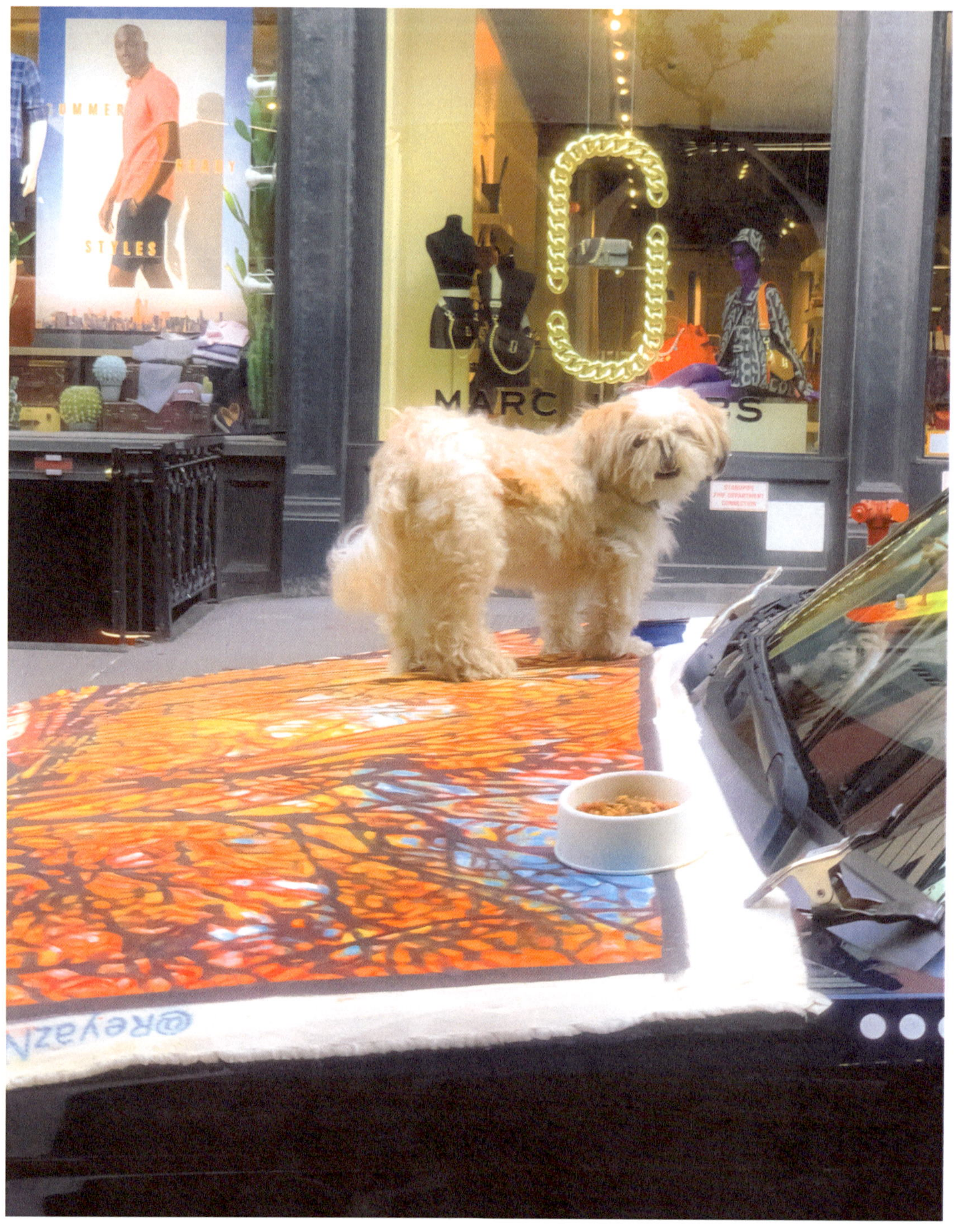

SUMMER
READY
STYLES
MARC JACOBS
@Reyaz

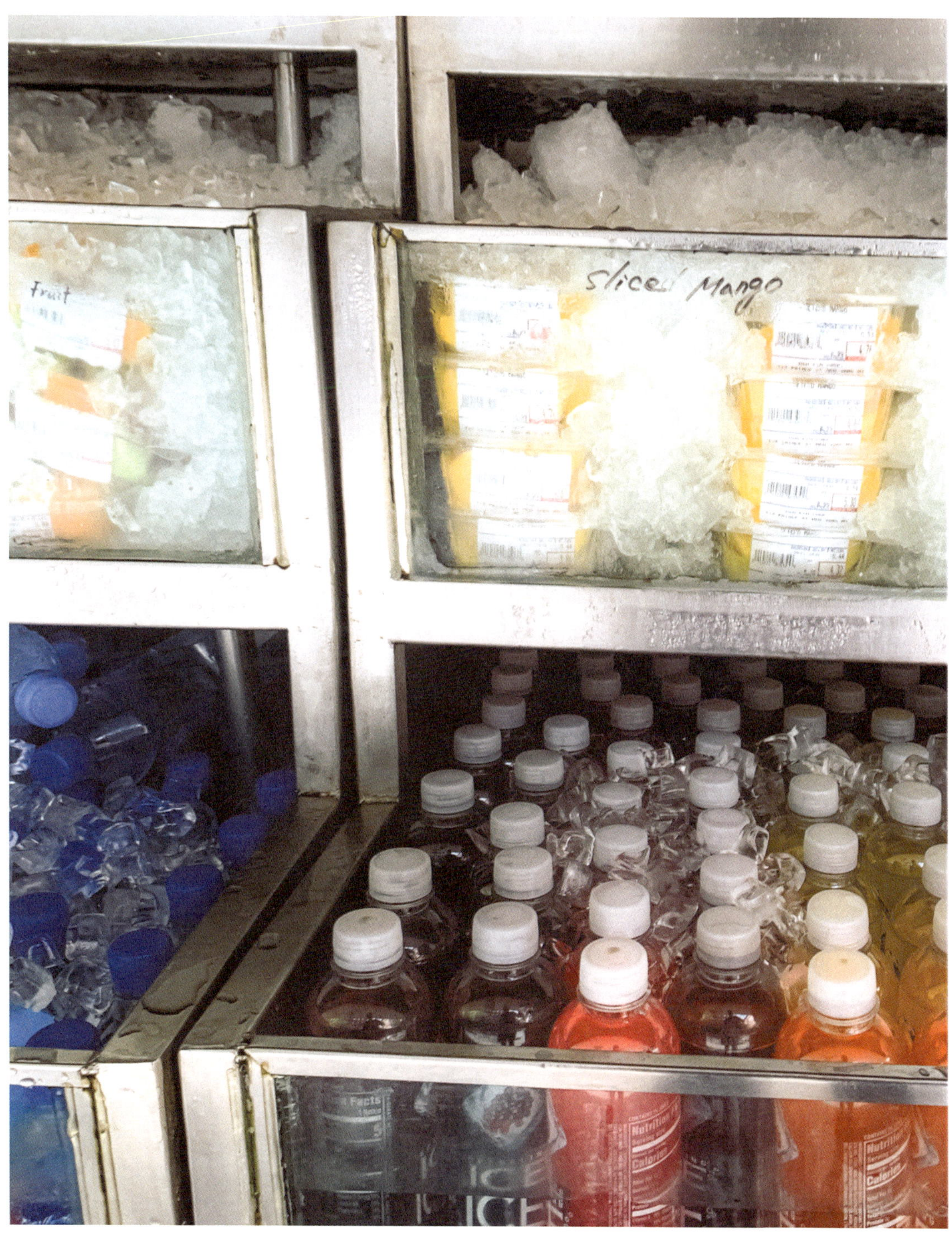
Fruit
sliced Mango

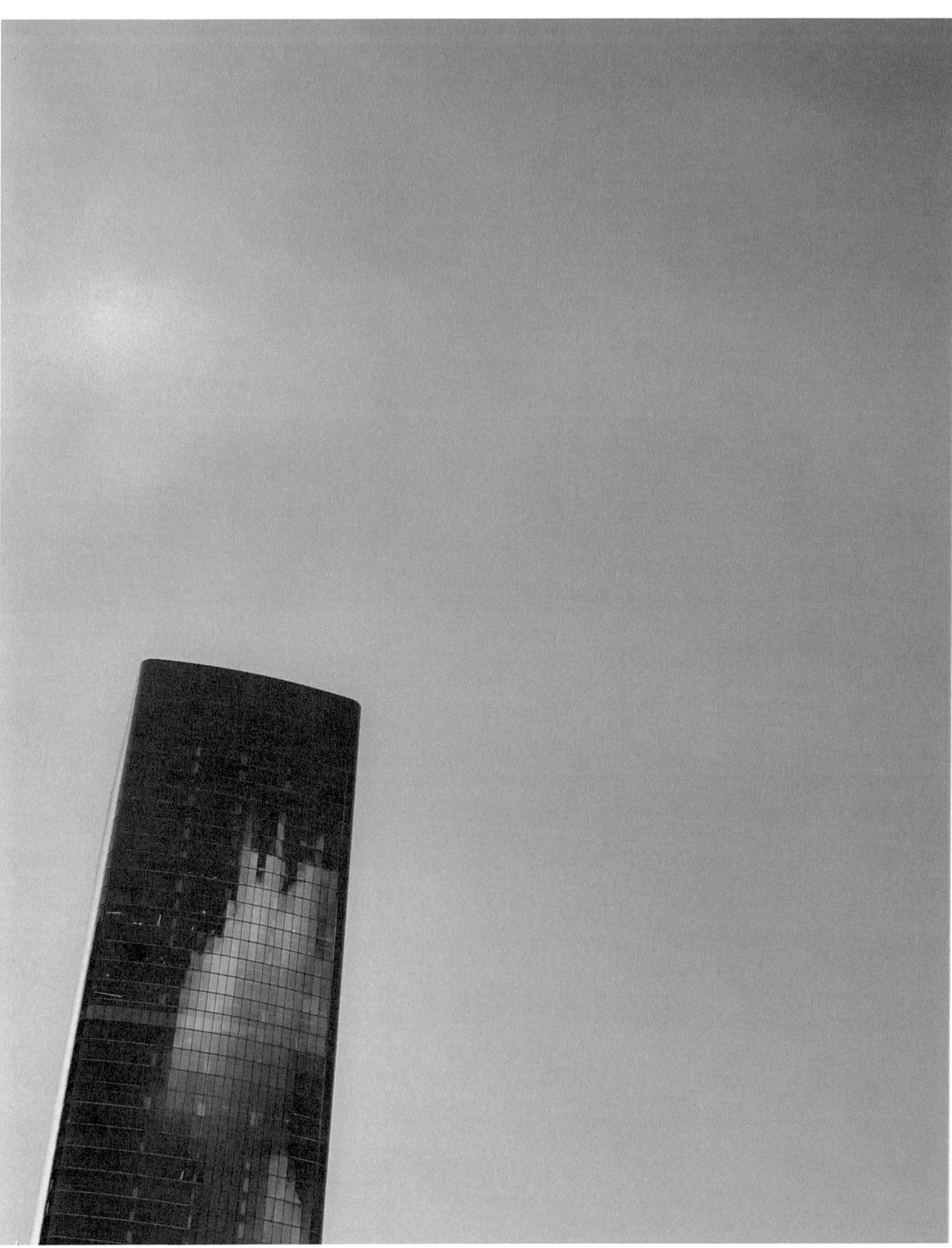

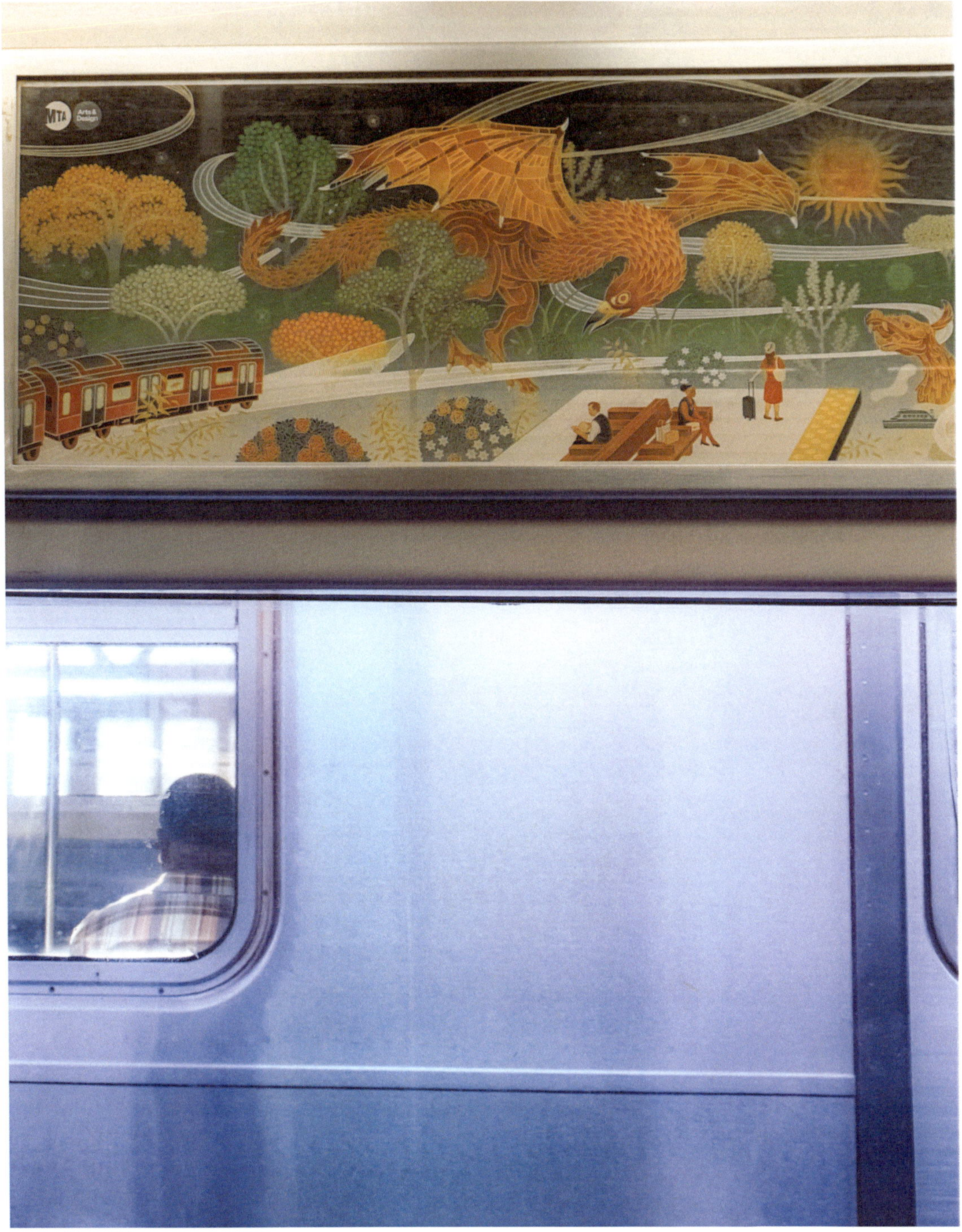
MTA
Arts &
Design

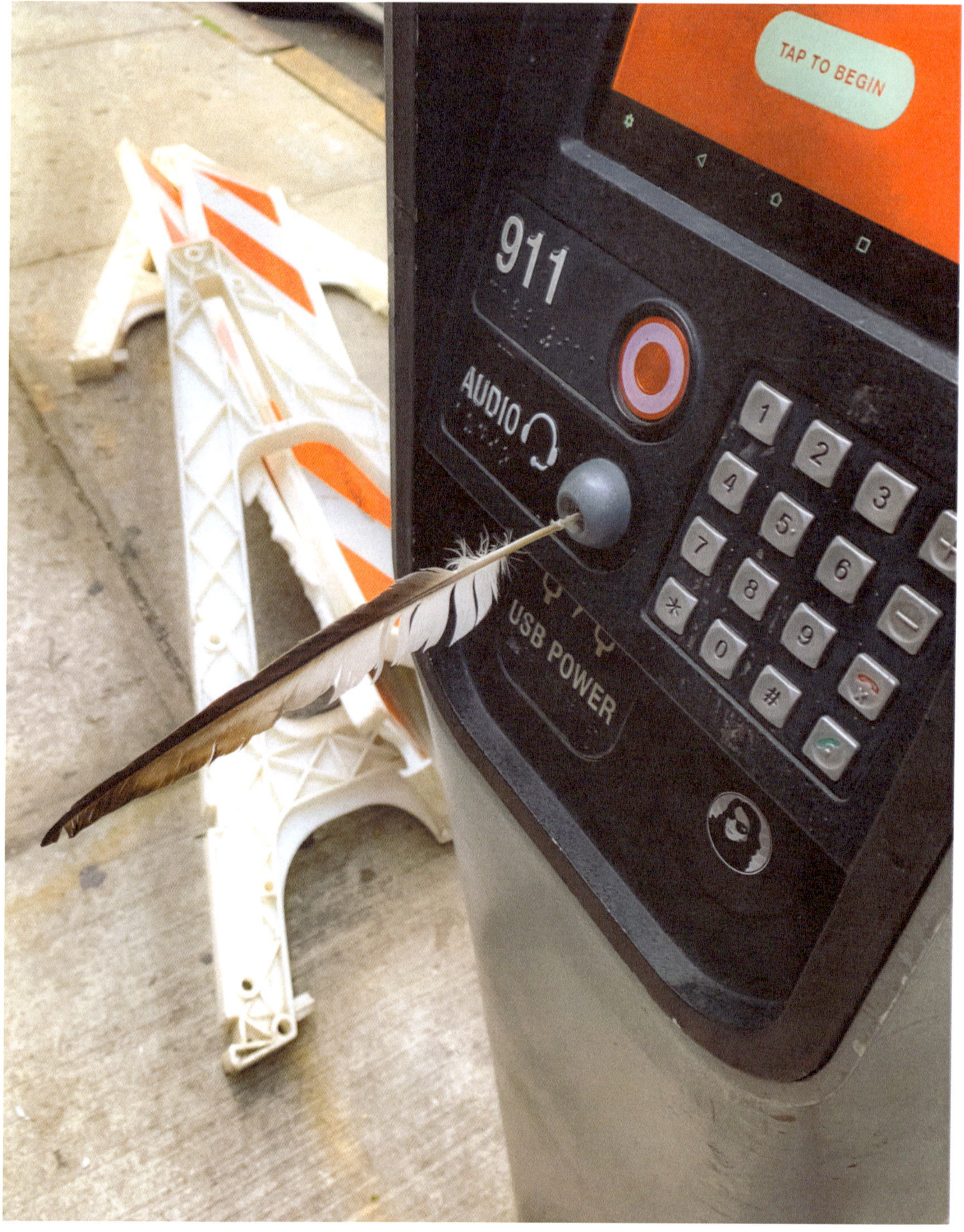

TAP TO BEGIN
911
AUDIO
USB POWER

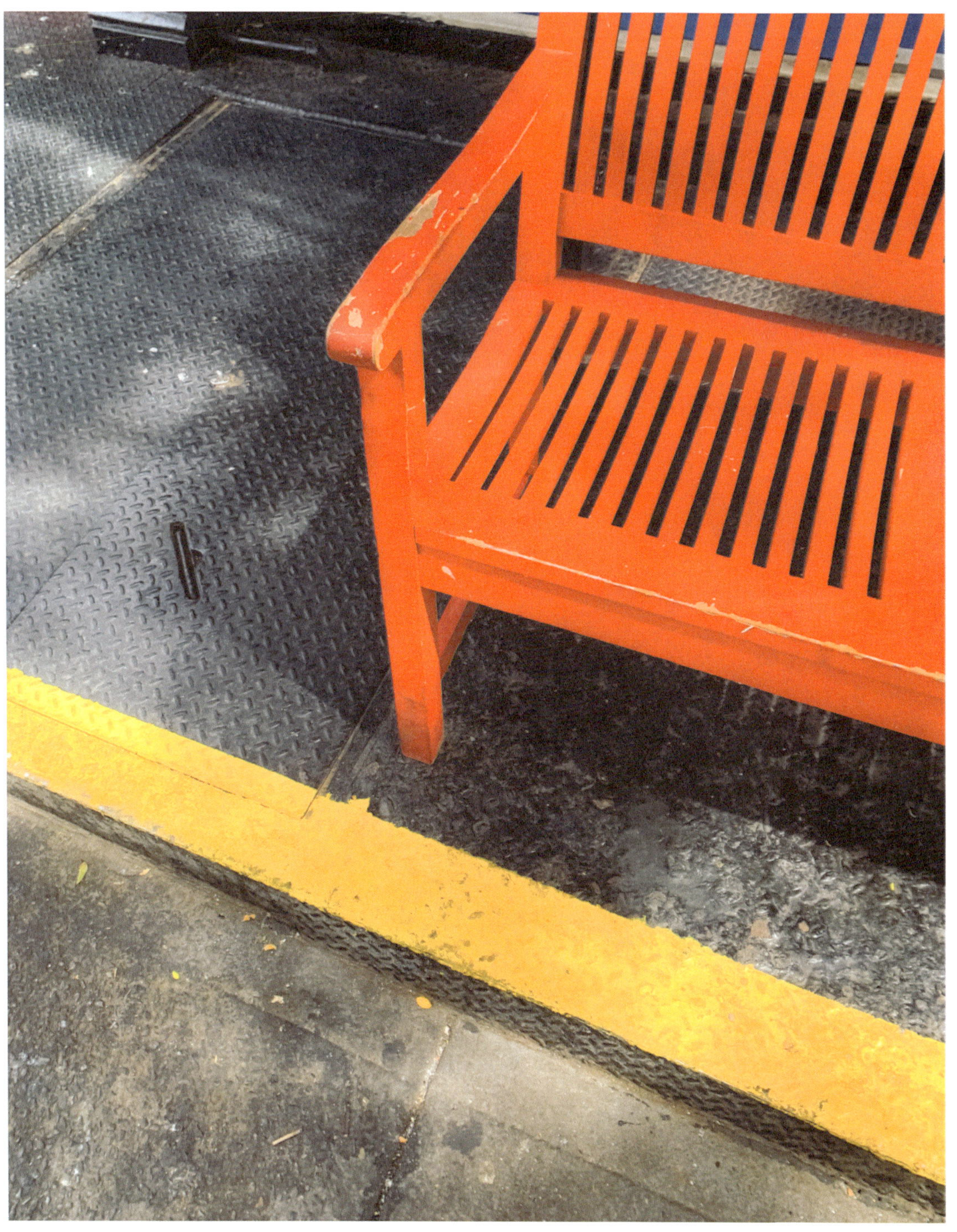

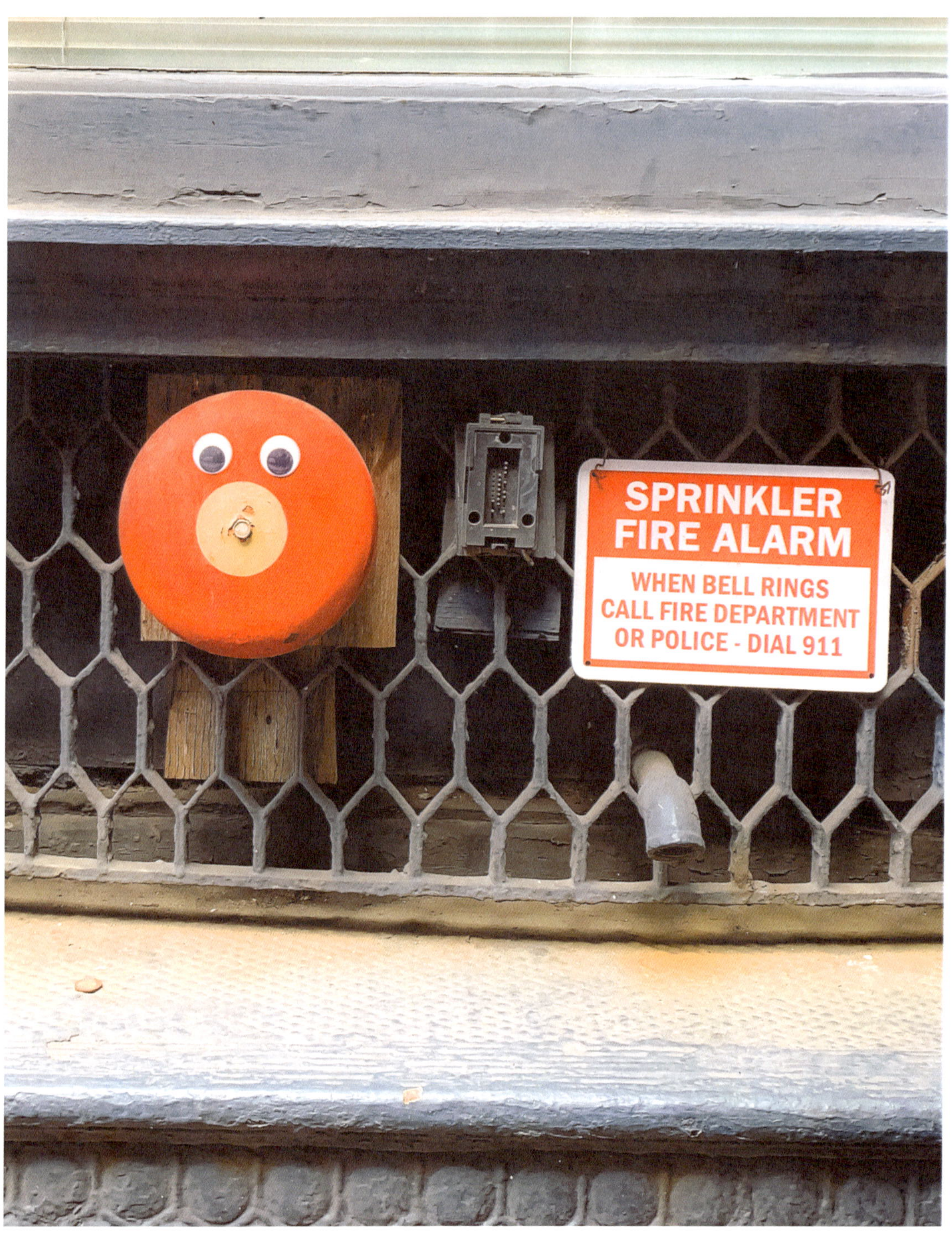
SPRINKLER
FIRE ALARM
WHEN BELL RINGS
CALL FIRE DEPARTMENT
OR POLICE - DIAL 911

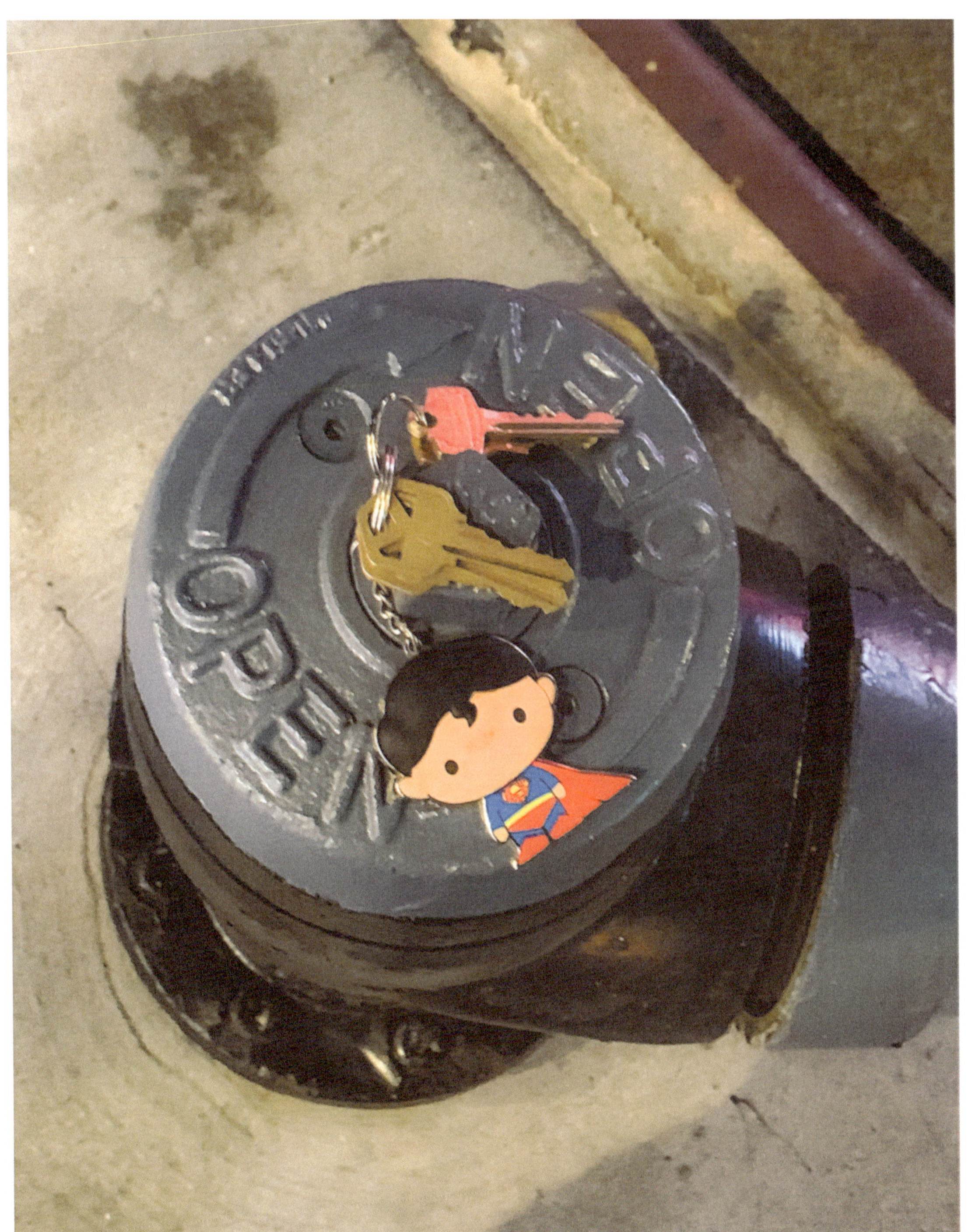
OPEN

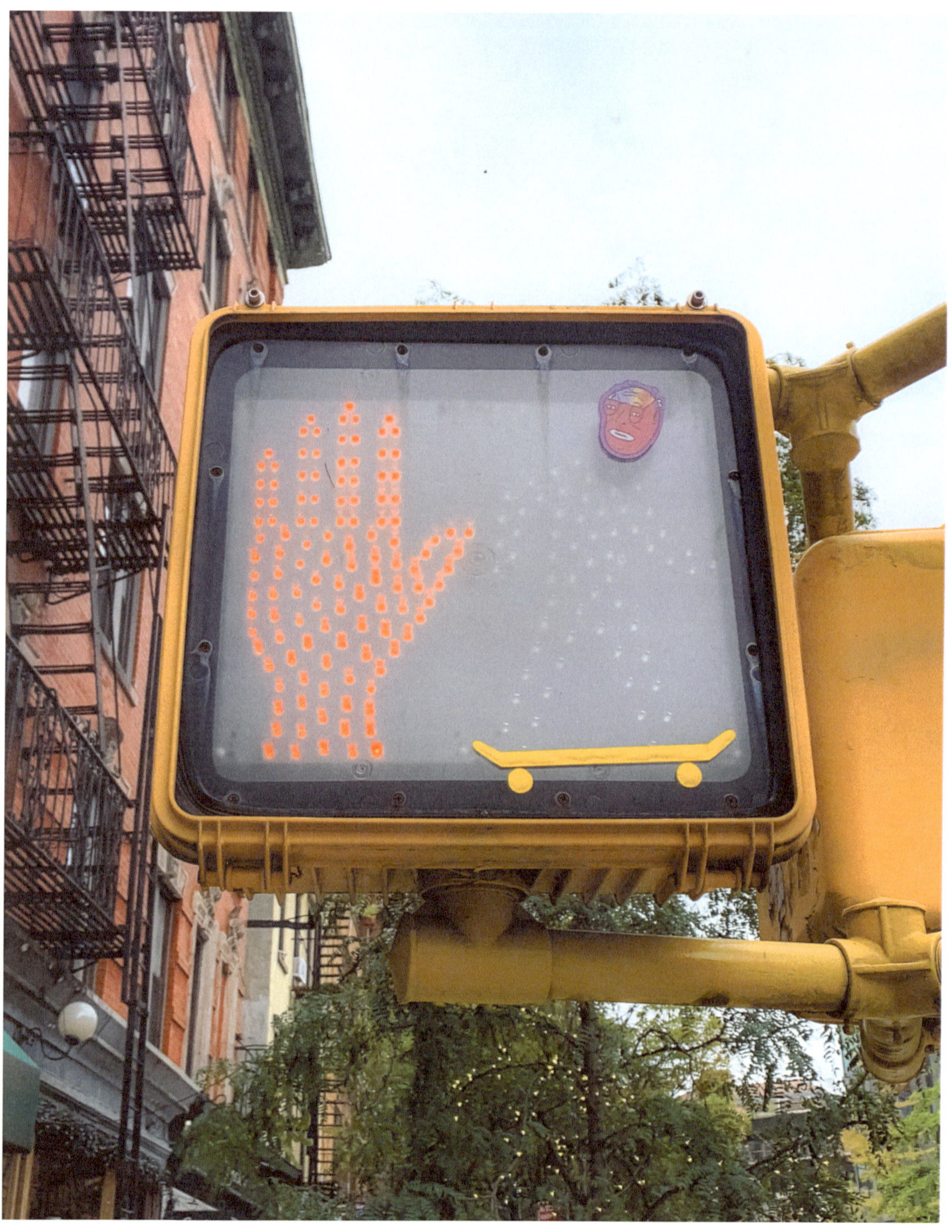

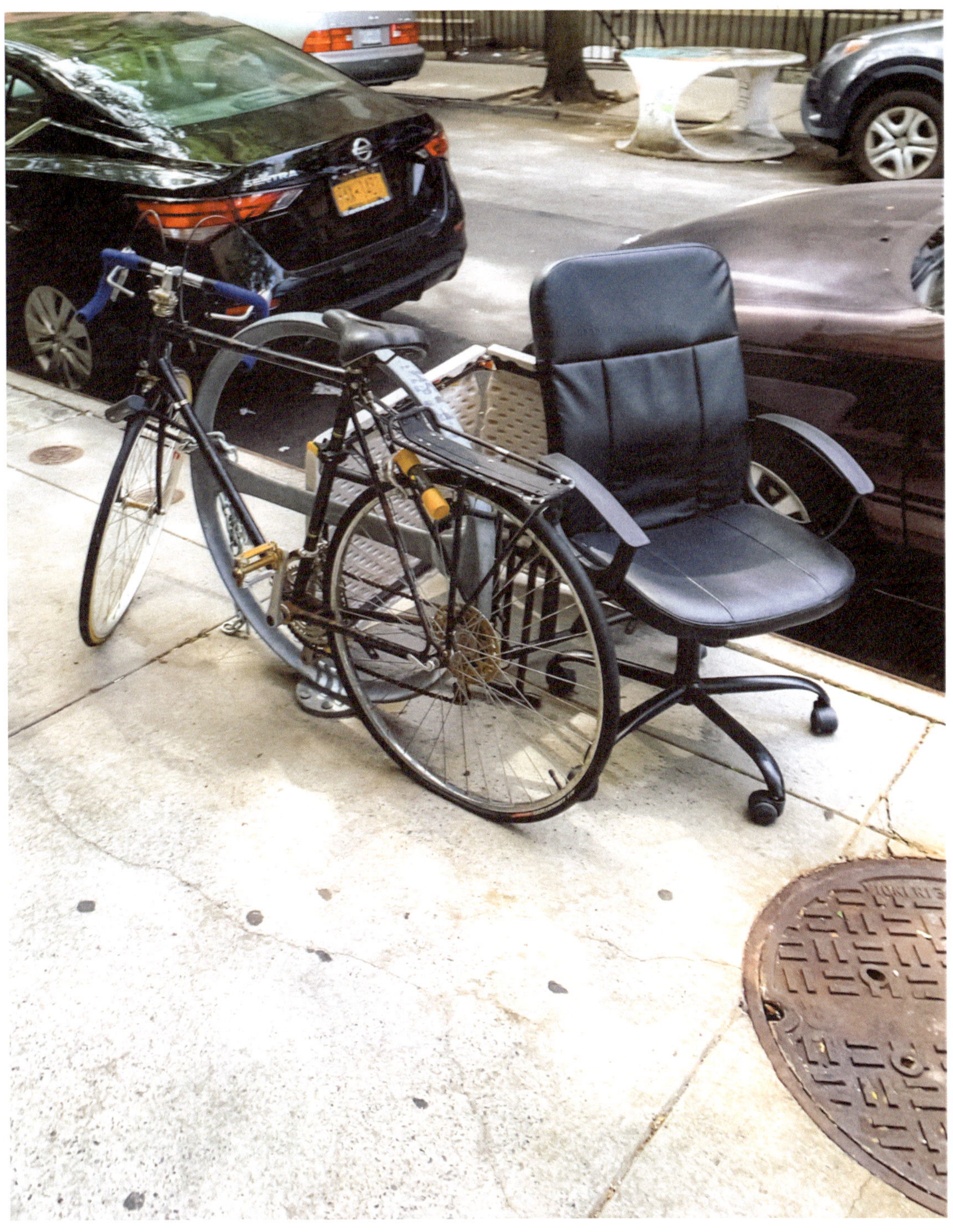

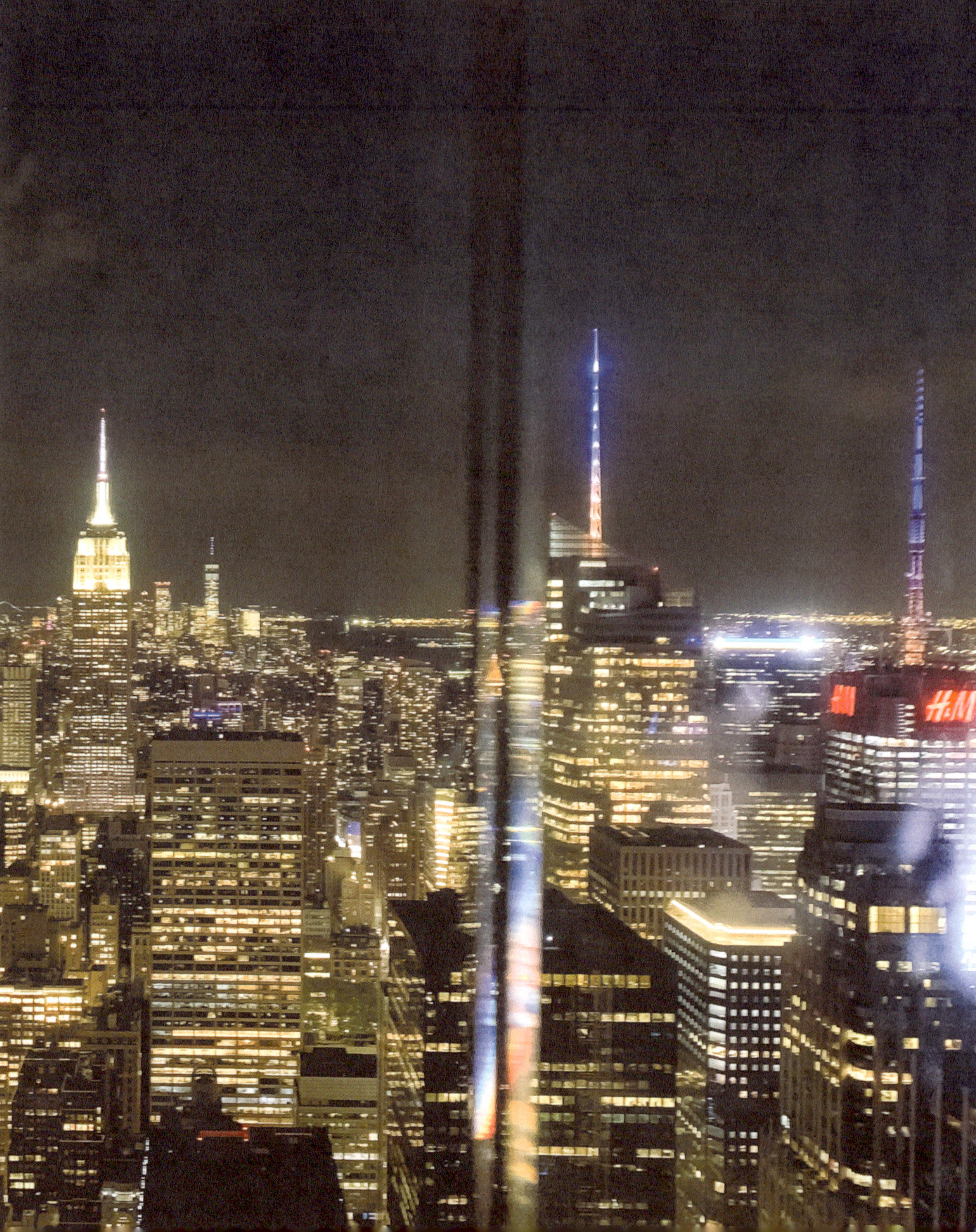
H&M
H&M